Walch Toolbook Series
Grammar, Mechanics, and Usage

A Comprehensive Guide to Usage and Style

Susan Stein

J. WESTON

WALCH
PUBLISHER

Portland, Maine

User's Guide to *Walch Reproducible Books*

As part of our general effort to provide educational materials that are as practical and economical as possible, we have designated this publication a "reproducible book." The designation means that purchase of the book includes purchase of the right to limited reproduction of all pages on which this symbol appears:

Here is the basic Walch policy: We grant to individual purchasers of this book the right to make sufficient copies of reproducible pages for use by all students of a single teacher. This permission is limited to a single teacher, and does not apply to entire schools or school systems, so institutions purchasing the book should pass the permission on to a single teacher. Copying of the book or its parts for resale is prohibited.

Any questions regarding this policy or requests to purchase further reproduction rights should be addressed to:

Permissions Editor
J. Weston Walch, Publisher
321 Valley Street • P. O. Box 658
Portland, Maine 04104-0658

Acknowledgments

The author wants to thank Bob for his technical help, but even more so for being the mainstay for this project (i.e., for watching the kids, cooking the suppers, doing the laundry, etc.); Maggie, Amelia, and Peter because they're such great kids; Margaret Cleveland, her editor, whose suggestions (and lunches) were helpful; the United Way of Greater Portland and their "weekend club" (especially Allison and Maree), and Portland Adult Education (especially Sandy) who let her use their computers; her friends who listened over and over again to grammar-talk; and to Donald C. Poppe, her high school English teacher, who first helped her fall in love with grammar.

Contents

Introduction

What you're holding in your hands, *Grammar, Mechanics, and Usage: A Comprehensive Guide to Usage and Style,* is not a stand-alone text for all your grammar needs. What it is could be even better.

Grammar, Mechanics, and Usage is a review book: a quick-reference, encyclopedic approach to everyday problems you have in the classroom. This text is meant to supplement your English classes in one of two ways:

1. If you're already using a grammar text but sometimes find you need more explanations, examples, and student worksheets, this book has them.
2. If your main focus is literature and your students are having difficulty writing essays, this book offers solutions.

For example, if your students hand in a draft that contains not a single comma, turn to Chapter 4 and review the comma section with them. Use this book and its easily reproducible student pages to hit again all those issues the big grammar book covers.

The underlying premise of this text is that few students out there will ask you to teach them about grammar. Let's face it, your typical student probably sees no need for the role of adverbs in life. Students don't want to learn grammar because it seems irrelevant—like leftover baggage from a bygone era that didn't have grammar software and spell check.

You don't have to convince them English is the bedrock of Western civilization. All you have to do is persuade them that proper grammar and usage offers them a language to communicate in when writing. I tell my students the challenge of grammar always reminds me of going to the garage with a car problem. I might explain the noise I'm hearing with words like "Well, the car seems to be taking a breath every time I turn a corner. It just seems tired." My mechanic politely nods his head, but inside I can hear him screaming, "TIRED? Your car is TIRED? Where's the problem, lady? With the clutch? The transmission? Give me something concrete." It can take us hours to figure out where the problem is even located because we're not speaking the same language. But if I walk in and say, "There seems to be a loud rattle coming from the rear axle," we're in business immediately.

You want to help your students to be better writers and thinkers; grammar does just that. It is the language writers use. So now all you have to do is remind your students there are millions of reasons for becoming proficient at writing. Whether they're writing thank-you notes, book reports, or phone messages, good grammar counts.

Each chapter of this book contains a two-page explanation for you describing the lesson that follows and suggesting extended activities to further drive home the point. Then there are some reproducible student pages offering a straightforward definition of what they are learning and some exercises to practice.

I hope this supplementary text will help make your job a bit easier while also giving your students some of the necessary "tools" for using the language we love. Once these basics become accessible to our students, they too can share our passion.

—*Susan Stein*

Chapter 1: Parts of Speech

Background Notes

You are about to begin something most students dread. Take that as fact one. So, your job is to try to present the parts of speech as something they want to learn. It is possible, but you must appear as excited as you want students to be.

Stress from the very beginning that grammar is *not* a science of memorization or a linear series of rules. Instead, it's the steady ground underneath a writer's feet. It's the string to the writer's kite. The goal of learning grammar should be to become better writers, not to become people who are good at doing worksheets.

What to Do on Day One

Find out what your students already know about the parts of speech. Together, brainstorm what the eight parts of speech are and then get a brief definition of each from the class. Most likely you'll get five of the eight with no problem, and your students will have no trouble giving you their textbook definitions. Now challenge their preconceptions (and tie in the myth that grammar is about memorizing rules). Show them, for example, that a noun can easily be changed into an adjective. Look:

- **Ernest Hemingway** is one of the best-known American authors of our time.

(No one in your class should have any trouble telling you that the boldfaced words are a noun since they name a person. That's correct in this example, but now watch):

- **Ernest Hemingway's** novels are some of America's best-known works.

(Now the same words—except for the 's—have become an adjective.)

If they don't believe you, show them how this happens over and over again with verbs turning into nouns and adjectives, pronouns into adjectives, and on and on. Turn this possible frustration into an advantage by showing how much freedom is gained by learning grammar.

With the possible exceptions of prepositions, conjunctions, and interjections, it doesn't help to memorize words as specific parts of speech. From your first opportunity, emphasize that learning good grammar is just a way to give you options as a writer. It's sort of like learning that the library is not the only place to go when you need to do research. The Internet with its Web pages may give the information you need. Once you see that a verb can be turned into a noun, you give yourself all sorts of new ways to construct your sentences.

Especially for ESL

Grammar is often a place where your ESL (English as a Second Language) students shine. Take advantage of that. Have them talk about their own languages and share similarities and differences. For example, have your Russian students explain how there are no articles in their language and see if you can get your North American students to explain how and where we use articles. (If you get the answer, please call

(continued)

Chapter 1:
Parts of Speech (continued)

me immediately. I've been looking for a way to explain them for years.) Have your Asian students show how they express verb tense; e.g., *I go store yesterday.* Then see if your native-language students can show how English verb tenses work before looking at the lesson on verbs. When going through the following worksheets, I often pair up ESL students with native-language speakers and have them work together. Often they can teach each other more than we could no matter how beautifully crafted our lesson plans are.

Extension Activities

Encourage your students to become grammar detectives. Have them bring in sample sentences from newspapers, novels, or even *TV Guide* entries and analyze them for how each word is being used. That's the key here. You want students to look at each word and see how it fits with the other words in the sentence. They need to have a solid grip on the definitions of each part of

speech, but more importantly, they should concentrate on the *use* of each word.

Another fun activity to punctuate this point is to give students five or six words and write a sentence or two for each, changing the word into a different part of speech each time. Possible words to use are: *drive, iron, ring, daily, right, that,* etc. This is especially appropriate after finishing up the last section of this chapter ("Same Word . . . Different Part of Speech).

One additional way to make the parts of speech seem more lifelike is to have each of your students "become" one of them. I make up a sentence (or use one from the student examples) and have each student hold a card with a word from the sentence on it in front of the class. Then she has to explain what part of speech she is and *how* she is connected to other words/classmates in the sentence. Sometimes I'll have students link arms to visually solidify the connections in the sentence. Students like this parts-of-speech drama.

Name _____ Date _____

Chapter 1: Parts of Speech

This is it! You are finally going to break the secret code about the eight parts of speech. Yes, you've heard it before and have wondered why it just doesn't seem to sink in, and yes, you may even wish it weren't necessary. But this time it will be different.

By the time you finish this chapter you're going to have a solid understanding of each part of speech. If you do all the exercises and ask your teacher every time you don't quite "get it," you will finally make sense of all those English-teacher words. For real.

Nouns

 A noun names a person, place, thing, or idea.

That's it. Often you can touch nouns (*chair, baby, rock*), but sometimes you can't (*freedom, love*). Occasionally they're capitalized (*Fenway Park, Senator Mitchell*); more often, they're not (*ship, bubble gum*). Every once in a while they name whole groups or collections of things (*faculty, committee, army*).

Exercise 1.1

Let's do some quick practice with nouns. In the following sentences, circle all the nouns.

1. Courtney walked through the Walt Whitman Mall.
2. A nation often stands behind its president in time of war.
3. The crowd went limp when the home team lost in overtime.
4. Democracy is often not appreciated by those who have it.
5. Only echoes of silence filled the auditorium.
6. One third of the staff voted in favor of the new contract.
7. The office files were destroyed in the fire.
8. Love can be a tricky game.
9. The lion tore across the savanna.
10. John felt pity for the bedraggled dog and brought the pooch home with him.

I bet you did just great. I bet you picked out all the nouns in those sentences. Now I bet you're just dying to know even more about nouns. O.K., I'll tell you. Here's what you need to know if you want *all* the facts on nouns:

Any noun can be put into one of five categories: common, proper, collective, concrete, or abstract.

Grammar, Mechanics, and Usage

Name _____   Date _____

Common Nouns: These are everyday people, places, things, or ideas that do not have to be capitalized.

Example	doctor, boatyard, soup, beauty
	In a quirky **turn** of **events**, the **doctor** called in sick.

Proper Nouns: These nouns name specific people, places, things, or ideas, so they have to be capitalized.

Example	Doctor Sampson, Joe's Boatyard, Campbell's™ Chicken Noodle Soup
	Doctor Sampson called in sick.
	(Now I have to capitalize the "d" in doctor and the "s" in Sampson.)

Collective Nouns: This is the fancy term for those nouns that name groups or collections of things.

Example	committee, platoon, gang, class, cast, panel, family, one half (it's part of a number)
	The **mob** went wild when the curtain fell after the **orchestra's** final **number.**
	(There is also one other noun in that sentence. What is it? What type is it?)

Concrete Nouns: Any thing you can touch, see, hear, taste, or smell.

Example	hat, car, Ring Ding™, chair
	The **dog** carried his **bone** to his **doghouse.**

Those three boldfaced words can be called concrete, common nouns. (If you're starting to feel that knot in your belly, relax. A few minutes ago you easily would have been able to pick those three words out as nouns, and that's what's really important. This stuff is just the technical details.)

Abstract Nouns: These are things you can't touch because they name qualities, characteristics, or ideas.

Example	determination, strength, courage, jealousy, love
	Truth is often in the words of the storyteller.

The boldfaced word is an abstract noun, and some would even call it a common, abstract noun. Can you circle the other nouns in that sentence and tell what type they are?

Now, go back to those 10 sentences on page 3. Above each noun write either common, proper, or collective, and then label them either concrete or abstract.

Don't worry, we're not done with nouns yet.

Name _____ Date _____

As you go through these lessons, you'll notice I keep stressing uses of words. Looking at the functions of words in a sentence is one of the tools to help you understand grammar better. While it's helpful and often necessary to be able to pick out a noun when you see one, it's most important that you see how the noun is working in the sentence. You need to know what job a noun has in each place in which it can appear in a sentence.

The Six Jobs a Noun (or Pronoun) Can Do in a Sentence

1. Be the Subject of a Sentence (You'll read more about this in the next chapter.)

Example	**Shirley** loves fruitcake. Two nouns here: Shirley and fruitcake Who or what is the sentence talking about? Shirley

So, here we say Shirley is the subject of that sentence. Then we could go on to further amaze and impress our teachers and say, "Shirley is the proper, concrete noun acting as the subject of that sentence, and fruitcake is a common, concrete noun."

2. Be a Direct Object

Example	Shirley loves **fruitcake.**

Same two nouns, but now we have a label for both of them. Fruitcake is receiving the action in this sentence; nouns that follow an action verb and answer the question who or what about the verb are called direct objects. Therefore, fruitcake is the direct object. There now, don't you feel better knowing more about that fruitcake?

3. Be an Indirect Object

Example	Shirley generously gave **Don** some fruitcake.

Now we know a little bit more about that crazy gal Shirley. She is still the subject of a sentence, and fruitcake is still a direct object. When a noun follows an action verb and it tells us to whom or to what something was done, we call it an indirect object. It's always located between an action verb and a direct object. Don is the indirect object.

Grammar, Mechanics, and Usage

Name _____   Date _____

4. Be a Predicate Noun

| **Example** | Shirley has always been a generous **person.**
 Two nouns: Shirley, person |

In this sentence, person is a predicate noun. That's the fancy name for a noun in the predicate part of a sentence that follow a "state of being" verb. You'll be reading about the predicate in the next chapter.

5. Be the Object of a Preposition

| **Example** | Shirley bounced the fruitcake on the **floor.**
 Three nouns: Shirley, fruitcake, floor |

Even though you don't know about prepositions right now, you will by the end of this chapter, and it's helpful if you know now that a noun or pronoun is always the last word in a prepositional phrase. So, you'll just have to trust me for a moment when I tell you that *on* is a preposition and *floor* is the object of the preposition.

6. Be an Appositive

| **Example** | Shirley, a generous **woman**, loves fruitcake. |

The words in the middle of those commas are called an appositive. An appositive is a noun (or a phrase containing a noun) set beside another noun in order to explain or describe the first noun more. Appositive means "placed near or beside." The noun *woman* in this example is an appositive because it's in apposition to Shirley.

All of that is a lot to know. You shouldn't try to force your brain to get it all in there. Right now just practice recognizing nouns when you see them. The rest of this stuff is just laying the groundwork for more complicated grammar issues. When we get there, you'll be ready for them.

Name _____   Date _____

Pronouns

 A pronoun is the word used as a substitute for, or instead of, a noun.

The easy pronouns are the ones used in place of nouns talking about people—*he* instead of John; *them* instead of Sally, Dick, and Spot; *hers* instead of Susie's purse. The harder ones don't look as if they're talking about people, but if you think about it (O.K., if you stretch it a bit), they are. For example, the words *few, nobody, all, who, both,* and *one* refer to an actual body, either one or more. We're simply eliminating the names. The hardest of all are the pronouns that seem to have nothing to do with people. Usually, that's because they're taking the place of things, ideas, or other nouns used in the sentence. *Which, that, this,* and *those* might not look as if they are replacing a noun, but they are. Below is a list of the six kinds of pronouns and their most common examples. Don't bother memorizing the lists, but do make a note of words you wouldn't normally think of as pronouns.

Personal Pronouns and Their Possessive Forms

These are pronouns that clearly refer to a person or something the person might own.

I, me, you	**he, him, she, her**	**it, we, us**	**they, them**
my, mine, your, yours	**his, her, hers**	**its, our, ours**	**their, theirs**

NOTE: Some of these pronouns are singular and refer to only one person; others are plural and refer to more than one person.

This might seem obvious now, but later on it becomes important that you can see which pronouns are singular and which are plural.

Reflexive and Intensive Pronouns

These are the personal pronouns with either *-self* or *-selves* added on the end.

myself, yourself, himself, herself, itself, ourselves, yourselves, themselves

NOTE: Use these pronouns in one of only two ways:

1. When referring to the noun that is the doer in a sentence.

   Lucy loves **herself**.

2. To intensify or emphasize the noun.

   Lucy **herself** is a blatant show-off.

Relative Pronouns

These are pronouns that introduce subordinate or dependent clauses.

who, whom, which, that, whose

We'll look at clauses in Chapter 2.

Grammar, Mechanics, and Usage

Name _____   Date _____

Interrogative Pronouns

These are pronouns used to ask questions.

who, whom, which, what, whose

NOTE: This list looks almost exactly like the one before, right? Again, don't worry so much about knowing which pronoun fits into which category. The categories change depending on how the pronoun is used in the sentence. What's important is just knowing a pronoun when you see one.

Demonstrative Pronouns

These are pronouns you would use when you're pointing something out, or demonstrating where something would be.

this, these, that, those

The Most Common Indefinite Pronouns

These are the tough ones, and we English teachers cop out by just saying these are the pronouns that don't fit into any other category. In other words, these are the words we know are pronouns based on their use in a sentence, but you might not think they were pronouns simply by looking at them. This is the list you might want to commit to memory.

all	anyone	everybody	most	no one	some
another	both	everyone	neither	one	somebody
any	each	few	nobody	other	someone
anybody	either	many	none	several	such

Something to Think About: The noun a pronoun refers to (or takes the place of) is called its antecedent. In the sentence *The storm lost its impact when it hit land*, "storm" is the antecedent for the pronouns *its* and *it*. Sometimes the antecedent comes in the sentence before the one in which the pronoun appears: John is a good friend of mine. *He* is always available to me. "John" is the antecedent to *he*.

Grammar, Mechanics, and Usage

Name _____   Date _____

Exercise 1.2

Directions: In the sentences below, circle all the pronouns. When possible indicate the antecedent to a pronoun by drawing an arrow to it. Then go back and underline all the nouns just to be sure you haven't forgotten what they are.

1. The people who moved here were originally from Alaska.

2. Many from the cast of a recent film portrayed themselves.

3. I would wear my blue shirt if only I could find it.

4. Which one of the new students lives near you?

5. She wishes her sister would move out already.

6. Most of Harvard's graduating class want each other to succeed.

7. Do you know the woman whose purse was stolen?

8. People who have never used the Internet are often afraid of it; others, like me, embrace its possibilities.

9. Each of the students brought a notebook on the first day of class.

10. Few of the cars on today's highways are new.

11. Everyone agrees snowboarding is the new rage on the slopes.

12. Cecelia met her husband at the airport.

13. The copy of the magazine that I read was from the local library.

14. Printers for computers are costly; however, they are often necessary for people who use them every day.

15. Either one of the children will go to camp.

More Complex Pronoun Issues

Now that you can recognize a pronoun when you see one, it's time to tackle the real issues surrounding pronouns. It's the teacher-talk you hear. Here's how it goes:

A pronoun must agree with its antecedent in person, number, and gender.

AND

You need to learn the case forms of pronouns and the uses of each.

Makes no sense, right?

Well, we're going to tackle it now, and soon it will be clear. The good news is we're going to forget about the first statement until Chapter Three, so don't worry about it for now. The second statement is actually not that difficult to get. Let's try.

Have you ever written a sentence and weren't sure whether you should use *us* or *we*, or *he* or *him*? That's because you didn't understand cases of pronouns, but no longer. Personal pronouns fall into one of three cases (think of that as a fancy way of saying categories). These cases are either *nominative*, *objective*, or *possessive*. Each of

Name _____   Date _____

these cases refers to the way a pronoun is used in a sentence. (Didn't I tell you I'd be stressing that over and over again?) Below are the pronouns detailed in each case. Memorize them and then we'll look at what the function of each case is.

	Nominative Case	**Objective Case**	**Possessive Case**
singular	I	me	my, mine
	you	you	your, yours
	he, she, it	him, her, it	his, her, hers, its
plural	we	us	our, ours
	you	you	your, yours
	they	them	their, theirs

Notice that *you* and *it* don't change their forms, so forget about them. Then let me assure you, you'll never have trouble with possessive-case pronouns either, since they are just the words we use to show ownership. The only tricky thing you should notice is that pronouns of ownership don't use apostrophes. Other than that, possessive-case pronouns offer no major problems.

Now, let's define what nominative case and objective case really mean.

You remember when we learned the six jobs of a noun? Well, here's where it matters. If a pronoun is the subject of a sentence or is in the predicate part of a sentence with a linking verb, you use a nominative-case pronoun. If a pronoun is being used as a direct object, indirect object, or object of a preposition, use a pronoun from the objective-case list. Think about this:

Which one of the following options is correct?

(Between you and I—OR—Between you and me,) I think someone's deodorant isn't working.

In the sentence above, the word "between" is a preposition (you'll be learning about them in just a few pages; for now, take my word for it). Therefore, you need a pronoun that acts as the *object* of the preposition—one in the *objective case*. (Weren't those grammar wizards clever coming up with a case named for how the pronoun is behaving?) Now the answer is clear:

Between you and me, I think someone's deodorant isn't working.

Here's a tougher scenario:

Your phone rings. The caller asks, "Is Jane there?" Do you say "This is her," or "This is she," or (to avoid the problem totally) "You got her"?

The correct answer is "This is she," because in that sentence you have a pronoun in the predicate of a sentence following a "to be" verb. Of course there's nothing wrong with avoiding the problem totally and just saying "Yup." We're going to go into this problem in more detail in Chapter Three, after you've learned about action verbs and state-of-being verbs and the parts of a sentence.

Let's try a few now, but don't worry yet if it's still not crystal clear.

Name _____ Date _____

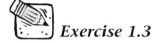

Exercise 1.3

Directions: In the following sentences, circle the correct pronoun:

1. She and (*I, me*) have been friends since kindergarten.

2. They blame (*us, we*) boys for everything that goes wrong.

3. When do you expect Lois and (*she, her*) to return?

4. Do not bother (*I, me*) or the driver while we're concentrating on the road.

5. How long did you work with (*they, them*) and Brian?

Grammar, Mechanics, and Usage

Name _____ Date _____

Verbs

 Verbs can be one, two, or even three words that show action, or show how something is existing (often called its "state of being"). They also indicate the timing of a sentence or its tense. Every sentence must have at least one verb to be complete.

Those three sentences above may not appear to make sense on the surface, but take a deep breath, because you really do sort of know this already; you just need a reminder.

The easy verbs are the ones that show action: **jumps**, **screamed**, **will show**. You can actually see someone doing these things.

However, sometimes in a sentence a verb shows us the *condition* a noun or pronoun is in. For example:

The police officer **looked** puzzled.

The police officer is not actively looking for something here. Instead, the officer's "state of being" is described—the way he or she *seems* to be. Look at this next example:

We **are** friends.

Again, no action is taking place, but a statement about the condition of several people is being made, and I can tell this is a condition that's happening right now because verbs also show us *tense*. We'll get into a complete explanation of tense soon enough, but first there's one more basic thing you need to be reminded of about verbs.

A verb is often more than just one word in a sentence—it can consist of two or three words all considered to be acting as the verb in the sentence. *Helping verbs* are the little words we have in English to help out the main verb. Be careful though; sometimes the helping verb isn't right next to the main

verb but instead is separated from it by other words in the sentence. In the examples below, the boldfaced words make up the complete verb:

Luisa **has been** in this country for only six months.

This desk **must weigh** 50 pounds.

Did you **ride** your bike all the way home?

Tony **should have become** a professional basketball player.

I **will** not **be swimming** on the school's team this year.

In English we often need more than one word to show the action or condition the subject is in and to indicate tense. You can also be sure that if a sentence is asking a question there's a good chance the helping verb won't be right next to the main verb. If you're having trouble finding the entire verb in a question, just rearrange the question into a statement and then you'll more easily be able to pick out the verb. For instance, the third sentence above could be made into a statement this way:

You **did ride** your bike all the way home.

Even though this doesn't make much sense as a statement, it does help you to find the complete verb more readily. On the following page is a list of common helping verbs to assist you in spotting one more easily.

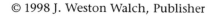

Grammar, Mechanics, and Usage

Name _____   Date _____

Common Helping Verbs

am	has	can (may) have
are	had	could (would, should) be
is	can	could (would, should) have
was	may	will (shall) have been
were	will (shall) be	might have
do	will (shall) have	might have been
did	has (had) been	must have
have	can (may) be	must have been

 Exercise 1.4

Directions: Just to prove to the rest of the world that you know a verb when you see one, underline each *complete verb* in the following sentences. Remember, several words can be acting together as the verb in a sentence.

1. The ball bounced into the street.

2. Because Maria was present at the scene of the crime, the police arrested her.

3. Julio ran towards the car because he was being chased by a grizzly bear.

4. Where are you going on vacation?

5. Eric should have been a father since he loves children so much.

6. David is a good photographer.

7. Will you come for dinner on Saturday night?

8. Shelby seems happiest when she is alone.

9. Galina had finally purchased the home of her dreams.

10. The arrow sped straight and true.

Hooray! You can spot a verb. That's good because now it's time to really start analyzing them.

Any word that acts as a verb is a dynamic word. Verbs can change from sentence to sentence depending on the timing of what you're writing about. In one sentence you may see the verb *paint* and you say to yourself, "God, I'm good. I can tell that's a verb because it's a word that shows action." Two days later you may see the words *has been painted*, and once again you pat yourself on the back because you were

able to remember that sometimes a verb is more than one word long. But you probably find you can't sleep at night until you figure out what the connection is between *paint* and *has been painted*. Well, worry no more.

Every verb has four parts to it: *infinitive, present participle, past,* and *past participle.* All other forms of the verb come from one of these. Both the present and past participles are always used with a helping verb. Let's look at some *regular verbs* (that just means verbs that don't have any weird quirks and

Name _____ Date _____

therefore are stable and dependable) and their four principal parts:

Infinitive	Present Participle	Past	Past Participle
work	(am) working	worked	(have) worked
explore	(am) exploring	explored	(have) explored
seem	(am) seeming	seemed	(have) seemed
look	(am) looking	looked	(have) looked
live	(am) living	lived	(have) lived

Notice any patterns with regular verbs? All of these verbs form their past tense the same way: by adding *-d* or *-ed*. That's the easiest way to tell if a verb follows the regular patterns of English grammar.

Previously, the words *am* and *have* were given with the two participle forms, but that's just to remind you that any helping verbs—*am, is, are, was, were, has been, will be, have, has, had,* etc.—could be used with a

participle, assuming, of course, the helping verb makes sense with the noun or pronoun used. (In other words, we would never say *John am looking for a friend.*)

Irregular verbs are the ones that form their past and past participle in some other way. That's a vague way of saying that sometimes the past form is a whole new word and sometimes the word doesn't change at all. For example:

Infinitive	Present Participle	Past	Past Participle
swim	am swimming	swam	(have) swum
write	am writing	wrote	(have) written
hit	am hitting	hit	(have) hit

It's important for you to be able to recognize and know when to use the most common irregular verbs. Below is a chart of the most common irregular verbs. Since the present participle is always a helping verb plus a verb with *-ing* on the end, we're going to just omit it from the chart. The word

"have" has also been dropped from the past participle list since it remains constant with all the past participles. Refer to this chart (or better yet, memorize this list) so you don't make common errors when describing an action or condition that happened in the past.

Principal Parts of Common Irregular Verbs

Infinitive	Past	Past Participle
arise	arose	arisen
awake	awoke	awaked *or* awoken
be	was *or* were	been
beat	beat	beaten *or* beat
become	became	become
begin	began	begun

Name _____   Date _____

Principal Parts of Common Irregular Verbs, *continued*

Infinitive	Past	Past Participle
bite	bit	bitten *or* bit
blow	blew	blown
break	broke	broken
bring	brought	brought
build	built	built
burst	burst	burst
buy	bought	bought
catch	caught	caught
choose	chose	chosen
come	came	come
cost	cost	cost
creep	crept	crept
deal	dealt	dealt
dig	dug	dug
dive	dived *or* dove	dived
do	did	done
draw	drew	drawn
dream	dreamed *or* dreamt	dreamed *or* dreamt
drink	drank	drunk
drive	drove	driven
eat	ate	eaten
fall	fell	fallen
fight	fought	fought
find	found	found
fly	flew	flown
forget	forgot	forgotten *or* forgot
freeze	froze	frozen
get	got	gotten *or* got
give	gave	given
go	went	gone
grow	grew	grown
hang (suspend)	hung	hung
hang (execute)	hanged	hanged
have	had	had
hear	heard	heard
hide	hid	hidden
hurt	hurt	hurt
keep	kept	kept

Grammar, Mechanics, and Usage

Name _____ Date _____

Principal Parts of Common Irregular Verbs, *continued*

Infinitive	Past	Past Participle
know	knew	known
lay (to put)	laid	laid
lead	led	led
lend	lent	lent
let (to allow)	let	let
lie (to recline)	lay	lain
lose	lost	lost
read	read	read
ride	rode	ridden
ring	rang	rung
rise (to get up)	rose	risen
run	ran	run
say	said	said
see	saw	seen
set (to place)	set	set
shake	shook	shaken
shoot	shot	shot
shrink	shrank	shrunk
sing	sang	sung
sink	sank	sunk
sit (to be seated)	sat	sat
speak	spoke	spoken
stand	stood	stood
steal	stole	stolen
strike	struck	struck *or* stricken
swear	swore	sworn
swim	swam	swum
swing	swung	swung
take	took	taken
teach	taught	taught
throw	threw	thrown
wake	woke *or* waked	woken *or* waked
wear	wore	worn
write	wrote	written

Believe it or not, that is not the complete list!

At this point, you may be feeling like the irregular verbs are more common than the regular ones. Or you may be feeling

Grammar, Mechanics, and Usage

Name _____   Date _____

outrage at whoever the genius was who came up with all these exceptions to the rule. I don't blame you. There's no good reason for all these convoluted verb forms. Just remember, you can always go to a dictionary and look up a verb in its infinitive form. It will list right there any irregu- larities, and if nothing is listed you can be sure you have a regular verb. (I have never been able to keep *lie* and *lay* straight and constantly have to refer to a dictionary. This is coming from someone who lives for grammar, so don't feel badly if you need a dictionary sometimes. Everyone does!)

 Exercise 1.5

Directions: Let's practice with these irregular verbs. Edit the following sentences. First locate the verb and underline it. Then decide if the right form of the verb is being used. If it's correct as it stands, just write the letter C in front of the number. If it's not right, change the verb to its proper form. Remember, sometimes a sentence has more than one verb, so be sure you pay attention to *all* the verbs in each sentence.

1. Trudy has growed almost three inches in one year.

2. Whenever I get the urge to exercise, I lay down until it disappears.

3. She could not have fell more than two feet, but she acted as if it was 20.

4. The burglar must have brought popcorn with him, because I found kernels right next to the spot where my television should have been.

5. Moon was convinced someone had stealed her bicycle.

6. The team swam at least 10 laps as a warm-up before practice.

7. Had I known you had such big biceps I would have gone out with you much earlier.

8. Beth could have took Bill to Disney- land two years ago, but she wanted to watch the excitement built.

9. I seen this movie twice before.

10. To get a better grade on your essay you should have wrote much more than three paragraphs.

11. My mother always hung her laundry out to dry.

12. I begun to think you had forgotten me.

13. The therapist have so many problems in his own life that he don't know how he can help anyone.

14. Modibo asked his wife if she had did the dishes yet because he wanted to help her.

15. Carlos claimed he couldn't go to the dance because he had drank a bad soda that upset his stomach, but Martha suspected the truth.

Now that you have a grasp on the four parts of any verb, it's time to look at what those parts do. The form a verb is in will tell you its *tense*. All tense means in relation to verbs (and not the way you may be feeling when we talk about verbs) is timing. The tense tells the time of the action or condi- tion being described. Let's take a look at the six tenses we get to play with in English:

Name _____   Date _____

The Simple Tenses

1. Present Tense—This tells us something is happening right now.

Example	I **see** a squirrel in the backyard.

However, it is more often used to describe actions or a state of being that happens over and over again.

Example	C.J. **teaches** word processing skills to her students.

Probably the most-used present tense verb is the irregular verb *be*.

Below is the conjugation of the verb. This is one you have to know:

I am	We are
You are	You are
He, She, It is	They are

2. Past Tense—This tense describes something that has already occurred and is over and done with. Regular verbs in the past tense end in *-ed*.

Example	Alba **graduated** from college in the Sudan.

3. Future Tense—This time frame describes an action or a state of being that hasn't happened yet, but will. You must use the word *will* or *shall* to express this tense. Use *will* before the verb except in questions. For the first person (I, we) in questions, use *shall* before the verb.

Examples	Elin **will cry** when her parents leave her with the babysitter.
	Shall we dance?
	Will you hike up Everest?
	(Just for future reference, the word **shall** is being used less and less, so feel free to just use **will** to express the future tense.)

The Perfect Tenses

The perfect tenses let us express more complicated time issues with verbs. You probably think our language is pretty easy; something either is happening now, happened in the past, or is going to happen. The truth is, our language is a complex web of timing. Sometimes we're talking about something that is starting right now, but will finish later on. Sometimes we need to show that something started in the past and is continuing to the present. The perfect tenses let us do that. Verbs in this tense have a form of the verb *have* plus the past participle.

Name _____ Date _____

4. Present Perfect—This tense allows us to write about things that started sometime in the past and have continued to the present time. It also expresses actions that were completed at some indefinite time in the past. Use *have plus the past participle form of the verb* with all persons except the third person singular, where you need to use *has*.

Examples	I **have rented** a snow board for our trip. (We don't know when exactly, but it has been done already and the snowboard can still be used.) He **has listened** (present perfect) to my side of the story and **knows** (present) I'm telling the truth. (Even if the story was told to him six weeks ago, he still believes it now.)

5. Past Perfect—This tense is a bit tricky because it really involves two periods of time in relationship with each other. You use it when you're describing an action or condition that was already over by the time some other past event occurred. The other reason you use it is to describe an action already completed at an exact time in the past. It is formed with *had, plus the past participle of the verb.*

Examples	By the time we **arrived** at the wedding reception, the cake **had already been served.** (There are two time frames here. The first boldfaced verb tells us these people got to the reception late and the second tells about what they missed because of their tardiness.) The keynote speaker **had finished** his address by 11:00 A.M. (This speaker's remarks were done by a specific time.)

6. Future Perfect—This tense is used when an action that began at any time will be completed sometime in the future. It is formed with *will have* or *shall have.* (Again, the use of the word *shall* is being phased out.)

Example	Next year Irving and Blanche **will have known** each other 50 years.

Grammar, Mechanics, and Usage

Name _____   Date _____

Progressive Tenses

Each of the above six tenses can be made into progressive forms. This tense describes actions in progress. The simple tenses form their progressives with a form of the verb *be and a present participle verb.* The perfect tenses use the same, *plus a form of the verb have.*

Examples	
	Present Progressive
	I am driving, writing, being
	he/she/it is driving, writing, being
	you, we/they are driving, writing, being
	Present Perfect Progressive
	I, you, we/they have been driving, writing, being
	he/she/it has been driving, writing, being
	Past Progressive
	I, he/she/it was driving, writing, being
	you, we/they were driving, writing, being
	Past Perfect Progressive
	I, you, he/she/it, we/they had been driving, writing, being
	Future Progressive
	I, you, he/she/it, we/they will be driving, writing, being
	Future Perfect Progressive
	I, you, he/she/it, we/they will have been driving, writing, being

The hardest thing about tense is trying to explain it. If you've been speaking English all your life, you probably already have good tense sense. You just naturally know all the distinctions of tense usage, and you never think about what the tense is implying. You just know how to do it. Look at the difference between the following:

Nicki went to Columbia for two years.

AND

Nicki has gone to Columbia for two years.

The difference seems so slight that frankly, you don't see much of one. Yet you do know what that difference is even if you can't explain it.

Name _____   Date _____

If, however, your first language is not English, go easy on yourself. This part of learning a new language is the toughest to get right since adding little things to the end of a verb like *-ing* really does change the meaning just a bit. Give yourself a break. This will come in time; just keep practicing. Don't worry about memorizing the definitions of and recognizing the differences between the perfect and the progressive tenses. Just try to be sure your writing and speaking expresses the timing you're going after.

No matter how long you've been using English here's a little tip on verb tense any writer can use: If you're writing an essay, story, term paper, or magazine article, KEEP THE TENSE THE SAME. Don't flip from past to present in the same sentence without a good reason. It confuses the reader.

 Exercise 1.6

Directions: First, find the verbs in the following sentences and underline them. Be careful; there are some tricky ones in a few sentences, and often a sentence will have several verbs. Next, think about the tense of the verbs and make any changes needed to correct the grammar.

1. Isaac taught her all she know about playing the clarinet.

2. Last summer my teacher advise me to get a tutor in chemistry.

3. The lives of animals in the rain forest has being in jeopardy for some time now.

4. Scientists predict many animals will had been extinct by the year 2020.

5. David will be participate this summer on the men's Olympic gymnastic team.

6. Mike had spoke to the surgeon about his mother's condition and was advise not to leave town.

7. Adam swim every evening in the summer.

8. Visitors to the museum are not suppose to touch any of the exhibits.

9. Roy is a regular comedian, but I can tell when he is get angry.

10. Arlene and Howard been in Egypt twice before their trip last October.

11. Marta and Kenny built their house on a hill overlooking a quaint town that settled in 1843.

12. Mrs. Falk will have been teach 35 years by the time she retires in June.

13. Yesterday I was ask to join a bowling league.

14. Marcel go to college after he gets his GED.

15. Amelia had always knew she want to be an artist someday.

Grammar, Mechanics, and Usage

Name _____   Date _____

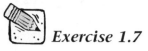

Exercise 1.7

Directions: Circle all the verbs in the following paragraph. Decide on a verb tense you want the paragraph to be written in and rewrite it. Keep the tense consistent throughout.

Above the office where I used to work was a karate studio. Every day as I go through my files, write letters, and fill out order forms, I could heard loud shrieks and crashes from the floor above me. All day long, the walls tremble, the ceiling shakes, and little pieces of plaster fall like snow onto my desk. Sometimes the noise really annoyed me; other times I decided to join in the pandemonium and blared a CD at top volume. When I am in a really bad mood, I stood on my desk and will pound out reggae rhythms on the ceiling with my shoe. Often on my way home from work I will see dazed people walking out the door with me. I find myself wondering why someone would volunteer to be thrown around for the sake of exercise.

Name _____   Date _____

Adjectives

An adjective modifies (or tells more about) a noun or pronoun. Adjectives answer the questions which, what kind of, and how many. *A, an,* and *the* are considered adjectives, but are sometimes referred to as "the articles."

Does that definition sound like three unrelated sentences to you? Or did you stop caring as soon as you read the word "modify" because you thought the English-teacher jargon was beginning? If you just let it sink in for a moment it will all make sense. Watch.

Take a sentence, any sentence. Pick out your nouns and pronouns, and then see if there are any words left that answer those three questions above. Here goes:

The three old men scratched their long beards.

The nouns and pronouns are easy enough to find, right?

Here they are: *men, their,* and *beards.* Now, let's use those three questions to see if there are any adjectives in there:

Which men? **The** men
What kind of men? **old** men
How many men? **three** men
What kind of beards? **long** beards

Before you say anything, I know you're thinking I forgot about the pronoun *their.* Doesn't it also answer the question, "Which beards?" Well, this is one of those tricky grammar places where we English teachers do some pretty fast talking. A little later on in this chapter you'll be reading about how one word can be used as many different parts of speech, and this is one of those times.

You have to think about how a word is *being used* in a sentence. What is each word's job? In that sentence above, you could call *their* a possessive pronoun (a pronoun showing a group of people who own something) or you could call it an adjective, since it describes *beards* a bit more. Frankly, it's not that important, but I think it's safe to say that when English teachers have coffee this is the kind of thing they talk about. They would probably conclude this is an example of a pronoun being *used* as an adjective. Clearly these people need more to do with their time.

Something to Think About: Did you notice that adjectives usually come right before the nouns they are describing? In English most often this is the case, but not always. Look at this:

My friends are interesting.

That word "interesting" is telling the reader more about "my friends" by answering the question "What kind of?" Therefore, it is an adjective. (You can impress your teacher by calling it a "predicate adjective," but remember, you don't want to cross the line into becoming a grammar geek, so be careful.)

Name _____   Date _____

Exercise 1.8

Directions: Now let's practice what you've learned about adjectives. First, put an N above all nouns and a P above all pronouns, since those are the words adjectives describe. Then circle each adjective and draw an arrow to the word it describes. Remember, adjectives answer the questions: Which? What Kind Of? How many? The first one is done for you.

1. The tired cleaning woman plopped her dirty rags in the metal bucket and started the long walk home.

   (*Her* can be called a possessive pronoun or a pronoun used as an adjective. You decide.)

2. Brittany likes soap operas filled with sultry heroines and swarthy men.

3. Ann's blueberry muffins and sincere kindness helped me when I was sick.

4. Out on the noisy playground the rambunctious children released their pent-up energy.

5. Many people stood in hour-long lines to finally have their chance on Disneyland's thrill ride, "Thunder Mountain."

6. Cuban cigars are often illegally brought into this country.

7. My aunt and his uncle are getting married someday.

8. A small child stood on the Mexican street corner begging tourists to buy small packs of Chiclets™ gum from her.

9. This laboratory experiment is fun.

10. Two loud crows woke me from my pleasant dreams this morning.

Name _____   Date _____

Adverbs

 Adverbs modify (describe) verbs, adjectives, and other adverbs. They answer the questions *where, when, how,* and *to what extent.* Many adverbs end in -ly.

Let's do what we did with adjectives. In the sentence below, first pick out any verbs or adjectives. Then we'll see if those questions work:

She is very quietly doing her rather difficult homework.

What's the verb? *Is doing.* Good. Any adjectives? You bet. That homework is described as *difficult,* so it's an adjective.

Now think about how each word is being used in the sentence and let's see if the questions help us find the adverbs:

How is she doing her homework? *quietly* (adverb modifies verb)

How quietly is she doing it? *very* (adverb modifies adverb)

How difficult is the homework? *rather* (adverb modifies adjective)

Exercise 1.9

Directions: Now you get a chance to really focus on adverbs. In the sentences below, put a V above all verbs and an ADJ above all adjectives since adverbs modify them and other adverbs. Then circle all adverbs and draw an arrow to the verb, adjective, or adverb they are describing. Remember, adverbs answer the questions Where? When? How? and To what extent? The first one is done for you.

1. Eduardo cautiously avoided the guards posted throughout the city and began his rather frightening journey.

2. The student ran home quickly.

3. Ly luckily landed a job with the state's largest insurance agency.

4. Mr. Nestleroth often returns to his very small hometown in Nebraska.

5. Finally, I accepted the reality that my father was never going to return home.

6. We went to a bean supper here last fall.

7. Kim gradually became accustomed to the warm winter in Kansas, but she never got over missing Alaska's cold.

8. Jason was a very smart boy.

9. Cece will soon return to Hawaii for a visit.

10. Ganya carefully unwrapped her birthday present and happily shared her candy with everyone.

Are you beginning to see that all these parts of speech have this cool connection? They all work together. Let's get some more practice to be sure it's making sense.

Grammar, Mechanics, and Usage

Name _____ Date _____

Exercise 1.10

Directions: In the sentences below, write N above any nouns, P above any pronouns, and ADJ above any adjectives.

1. Emilia's beautiful red hair flowed like a river down her back.
   (Something to think about: How is "her" being used here?)

2. Some runners take part in grueling marathons; others know it is something their bodies could never endure.

3. A loud, annoying dog lives next door to us.

4. The three thieves botched the nearly flawless burglary by taking off their ski masks in front of the security camera.

5. Ali described the grisly massacre in Pakistan.

Now put a V above the verb(s), an ADV above any adverbs, and an ADJ above any adjectives in the sentences below.

6. In New York people often wait in long lines at most department stores.

7. Eventually Jake and Olivia decided they would like visiting the rather interesting Orient.

8. Children generally like outrageous amusement parks, loud video games, and noisy rooms filled with heaping plates of junk food.

9. Hung's facial scar was barely noticeable.

10. Joan carefully and slowly cooked a delicious meal.

Grammar, Mechanics, and Usage

Name _____ Date _____

Conjunctions

 Conjunctions connect words and thoughts.

There are three types of conjunctions, and while it's not important for you to memorize the category each conjunction fits into, it is important for you to recognize a conjunction when you see one. Later on you'll be learning that certain marks of punctuation are often needed somewhere near conjunctions.

Coordinating Conjunctions

and	but	or	nor	for

Correlative Conjunctions
(These are used in pairs)

either . . . or	not only . . . but (also)
neither . . . nor	whether . . . or
both . . . and	

Commonly Used Subordinating Conjunctions

after	for	till
although	if	unless
as	since	until
as if	so that	when
as though	than	where
because	that	wherever
before	though	while

 Exercise 1.11

Directions: In the sentences below, circle all conjunctions.

1. Peanut butter and jelly is probably the most popular sandwich in American lunch bags.

2. I will either go to England or Ireland this summer.

3. Because money was always a problem, Shyla decided to go back to work full-time.

4. Neither Ryan nor Emmit had ever seen a hockey game before.

5. If you build it, will they come?

6. Bob was not only a good father, but also a good husband.

7. Charlene wanted to go to the movies, but she wasn't sure which one to see.

8. Nancy was late for work, since she forgot to set her alarm clock last night.

9. I wanted both whipped cream and nuts on my ice cream sundae.

10. Kevin will be dressed and ready for work before the sun comes up.

Grammar, Mechanics, and Usage

Name _____   Date _____

Prepositions

A preposition is a little word that shows a relationship between a noun or pronoun and some other part of the sentence.

The 42 Most Frequently Used Prepositions

about	around	between	in	round	underneath
above	at	by	into	since	until
across	before	down	of	through	up
after	behind	during	off	till	upon
against	below	except	on	to	with
along	beneath	for	over	toward(s)	within
among	beside	from	past	under	without

Another thing you should know from the start about prepositions: You should never see prepositions all by themselves; they always come with other words and form a *prepositional phrase* (see page 38). This is simply a group of words starting with a preposition and ending with a noun or pronoun (called the object of the preposition).

> **Example**   (Beneath the driver's seat) (in my car) is so much junk I'm surprised I haven't been arrested (for driving) an unlicensed garbage vehicle.

The words in parentheses are the prepositional phrases. All of those words act together as sort of measures of music and help give rhythm to your writing. Notice also that every prepositional phrase begins with one of those words on the above list, and ends with a noun or pronoun.

Something to Think About: While that list I gave with the 42 most commonly used prepositions hits the ones you'll see most often, it is not a comprehensive list. Also, some of those words on the list can be different parts of speech depending on how they're *used* in a sentence—sorry, but I have to keep stressing that point.

Which of the sentences below uses the word *under* as a preposition? How is the word *under* being used in the sentence where it's not a preposition?

1. The puppy is under here.

2. The puppy is under the table.

Grammar, Mechanics, and Usage

Name _____   Date _____

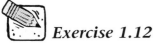 *Exercise 1.12*

Directions: Circle all prepositions in the sentences below. Then put parentheses ( ) around each entire prepositional phrase.

1. The two angry beavers who lived at the bottom of the dam were brothers.

2. Gidget and her boyfriend went to the beach with their surfboards under their arms.

3. My brother, who is about four years older than I, moved from Pennsylvania to California after graduating from college.

4. During the height of the blizzard, thousands of Coloradians had to survive without electricity for more than two weeks.

5. Around the corner from our house is a quaint little corner store.

6. By the time the operation was over, most of Cam's family had arrived at the hospital.

7. Ian wore the same ragged T-shirt every day except Sunday.

8. Kyle hit the ball over the river and through the woods, eventually giving his grandmother a concussion.

9. Downtown, beside the fish market, Donna hung out with her friends.

10. Andy was the only boy in school without a girlfriend, but he didn't seem to mind.

Grammar, Mechanics, and Usage

Name _____   Date _____

Interjections

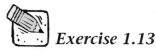 **An interjection is a word or words used to show strong emotion.**

These words have little grammatical relation to the rest of the sentence, and almost seem to be standing there as if to say, "Notice me, Notice me!" I suggest you use these words sparingly and find other words that really express the emotion you're going after.

Common Interjections

Wow!   Hooray!   Holy Bat Cave!   Gosh!   Gee Willikers!

You get my point?

Exercise 1.13

Directions: In the sentences below, mark C above any conjunctions, P above any prepositions, and I above the interjections.

(If you really want to razzle-dazzle your teacher, try to figure out what part of speech *every* word is.)

1. By practicing daily and studying on the weekends, Martin earned a coveted Juilliard scholarship.

2. Hooray! School is canceled due to snow and ice.

3. When Buddy passed his driving test, he didn't know whether he should tell his mother or his girlfriend first.

4. Yippee! Sharon and Mike are buying not only the tickets but also tonight's dinner.

5. At the end of the rainbow is a pot of gold.

Name _____ Date _____

 Exercise 1.14

Directions: Now it's time to put all that you learned to work for you. Put on your "grammar detective" hat again and concentrate on how each word is being used in the following sentences. Then above each word write what part of speech it is. Use the following as abbreviations: N for noun, PRO for pronoun, V for verb, ADJ for adjective, ADV for adverb, PREP for preposition, C for conjunction, and I for interjection.

1. The industrious student earned a top grade in the class.

2. That lively baby and his sister make life very hectic for their parents.

3. Whew! I am glad final exams are finished.

4. They knew immediately it would be a fun day.

5. Victor wanted a new job, but Maria feared he would never find a better one.

6. After he left Somalia, Dirte found he could not practice medicine in the United States.

7. She and I went home soon after the movie.

8. They usually get a raise in October.

9. Since Bob works during the day, he usually jogs at night.

10. Dozens of backpackers began the long trek through the Appalachians with their equipment on their backs.

Same Word . . . Different Part of Speech

Let's say just for a moment that everything you've read up to this point now makes sense. In fact, because you know the parts of speech so well you are considering a career as a grammarian. (Don't!) Let me remind you of a slight complication.

You cannot memorize words as specific parts of speech. In one sentence a word can be a verb, and in the next it's a noun. The same thing can happen with pronouns and adjectives, or nouns and adverbs. In fact, even those prepositions I told you to memorize occasionally act like adverbs or nouns.

Your first reaction is probably to throw up your hands and run screaming to the nearest math class. I don't blame you. However, consider for a second how neat it is having a language that mirrors our humanity. It changes just like we do. When you were seven you hated chop suey; now you crave it. Words change too, and that's part of what makes this all so much fun. Consider yourselves grammar detectives and look at each sentence as a mystery to solve. Think of how each word is being *used* in a sentence and that will help you figure out its part of speech. We'll keep hammering this point throughout the text, so don't fret.

Name _____   Date _____

Exercise 1.15

Directions: In the sentences below, indicate above each boldfaced word what part of speech it is.

1. "I **love** you," Romeo told Juliet.

2. His **love** for her was clear to all.

3. Peter's much-**loved** blanket was in shreds.

4. The trapeze artist flew **up** in the sky.

5. **Up** the street and around the corner there is a new store.

6. **These brown** books are outdated.

7. I want **these**.

8. **Brown** is my favorite color.

9. **Which** coat did you buy?

10. **Which** do you want?

Chapter 2: The Sentence

Background Notes

In the first chapter we were asking students to concentrate on individual words. Now we're shifting to look at groups of words. The goal is simple: We want our students to know what a sentence is. We also want them to think of words in clusters so they can see that some clusters make sense by themselves and some do not.

What to Do on Day One

I usually begin this unit by putting groups of words on the board. Then I have students tell me which groups make sense and which do not. Here are some word groups I've used. Notice, I try to vary the length of word groups, and I am sure to include punctuation in case any student thinks that's the sign of a sentence. I've also indicated for you whether groups are complete or incomplete.

1. Deep in the remote woods of Montana on the western side of the Rockies. (Incomplete)

2. March! (Complete—[You] march!)

3. While the sound of falling snow enveloped us. (Incomplete)

4. Riding a horse. (Incomplete)

5. She wept. (Complete)

Now you can begin a discussion of what is needed to make up a sentence. Students should easily be able to see it has nothing to do with length or punctuation, so try to pull in those words students

know—like noun, pronoun, and verb—to see if you can get closer to the definition of a sentence. Consider this:

She desires.

Is that really a sentence? Does it truly make sense by itself? If this sentence is read in the context of a paragraph outlining the subject's hopes and dreams, it probably would, but on its own the reader is left wondering exactly what it is she so wants. Some verbs in English just beg for an object.

Questions to Ask Students

Is it ever O.K. to have a phrase or clause stand alone in writing? Do authors ever use incomplete sentences? Why?

Especially for ESL

Most ESL students have no trouble with the concept of phrases and clauses, but since we're beginning to look at groups of words, here's where they often begin to have problems with syntax. Begin to emphasize word placement and some typical patterns in English: for example, adjectives often come before nouns, and prepositional phrases always end with a noun or pronoun.

Extension Activities

Let students have fun with groups of words. Have students work with classmates and give each set some interesting word groups. Then have them identify the word groups as either phrases or clauses. Now tell them to craft some clever sentences. Encour-

(continued)

Chapter 2:
The Sentence *(continued)*

age each group to drop the word clusters into different parts of the sentence, not just at the beginning. Here are some word groups you might want to use:

1. in the heat of the moment

2. who just won $1,000,000

3. even though it was no longer fun

4. during the long hours at the video arcade

5. without his shoes on

Chapter 2: The Sentence

You figure you've got this one nailed, right? You've been writing sentences for years and talking in them since you were two and a half. What could you possibly have to learn about the sentence?

My guess is lots.

Sometimes what *looks* like a sentence isn't, and what doesn't, is. Furthermore, knowing what each part of speech a word is won't by itself help you construct a full-fledged, honest-to-goodness, real-live sentence. You need to know what the parts of a *sentence* are so that every time you write a sentence it will be considered complete.

It's as if you're going to build a book-shelf and you have all the tools you need: wood, nails, hammer, and even a loose plan. But now you actually have to put them all together and build something that works. So that's what we're going to do. We're going to take our tools (words) and create something usable: solid sentences.

Before we even define exactly what a sentence is, let's look at what has to be in every sentence you write.

The Subject and Predicate

Every sentence has two parts: a **subject** and a **predicate**—every one, every time. If it doesn't, it's not a sentence. Let's look at each part:

 The SUBJECT is the *who* or *what* of a sentence.

 The PREDICATE is the *does what* or *is what* part of the sentence, which includes the verb and any words describing it.

I'll say it again: A sentence must have BOTH a SUBJECT and a PREDICATE to be complete. (But be careful, this is not the complete definition of a sentence . . . more on that soon.)

Look at this example:

The boy in the yellow raincoat jumped up and down in the large puddles.

Who or what? The boy in the yellow raincoat

Does what/is what? jumped up and down in the large puddles

Here's another example:

Urgently she lifted up the ax and hacked away.

Who or what? she

Does what/is what? urgently lifted up the ax and hacked away

Name _____   Date _____

And, yet another:

The tractor broke down in the middle of the field.

Who or what? The tractor

Does what/is what? broke down in the middle of the field

Now that we know what the parts of a sentence are, we can come up with a definition:

A sentence is a group of words that expresses a complete thought.
(That means it is a group of words that makes sense to most people, most of the time.)
It must have both a subject and a predicate to be considered complete.
(That means every sentence must have at least one noun or pronoun and one verb.)

This is English-teacher Philosophy 101. We are trying to make it look really hard to understand the definition of something as simple as a sentence, but, it's not really that tough. Simply put, don't rely on punctuation to make a sentence for you. Starting a group of words with a capital letter and ending with a mark of punctuation won't turn a group of words into a sentence. Make sure the words you're stringing together make sense even if they are pulled out of the context of the paragraph you're writing. To do that you need to make sure that *every time* you write a sentence you include a complete subject (a word or group of words that say who or what) and a complete predicate (another word or group of words that say what the "who" or "what" is *doing* or *is*).

Occasionally it may be hard to find the subject or predicate, but don't give up. Look at this example: *"Kiss me!"* Is this a sentence? It appears to be only a predicate, but this is an example of a sentence with a hidden subject. The implied subject is "you," (*You kiss me!*), and so this does fit our definition of a sentence.

Exercise 2.1

Directions: In the following sentences underline the subject once (and any words that describe the subject) and underline the predicate (and words that describe it) twice. Every word in the sentence should be underlined.

1. Clarissa diligently washed my red car.

2. Stop screaming.

3. Sen's memories haunted him even after leaving Vietnam.

4. The faculty and administration decided to impose a "no hats allowed in class" policy.

5. Why did the students object?

6. Rashid and Philip have been friends since kindergarten.

7. Recently I visited Mexico.

8. The last day of school is a reason to celebrate for most students.

Grammar, Mechanics, and Usage

Name _____   Date _____

9. Where were you born?

10. The fire chief and police officer worked together at the crime scene.

Notice anything? It looks as if every sentence in English starts with a subject followed by the predicate, unless it's a question. (In questions you usually have to rewrite the sentence as a statement to more easily find the subject and predicate. For example, #5 would be written as *The students did object why.* Even though that doesn't sound right, it does help to see what's the subject and what's the predicate. Once you've done that you also see that this really is another example of a sentence written with the subject first.) That is the usual format, but because we're a clever people, we try hard to mix that up a bit just to give variety to our writing. Read on.

Name _____   Date _____

Phrases

Up to now we've pretty much been looking at individual words, although if you've been reading carefully you probably noticed how often I try to get you to think about the connections between words. That's because many sentences have groups of words acting together to further explain the subject or predicate. Let's start learning the technical definitions for these clusters of words.

> **A PHRASE is a group of words that acts as a unit. The unit acts as a noun, an adjective, or an adverb. A phrase does not have both a subject and a predicate.**

What I think is most important about that definition is that you never think of a phrase as a sentence. Sometimes it looks as if a phrase has a subject or a predicate, but the key is it doesn't have *both*, so it can never stand alone as a sentence. Instead, it's just part of a sentence that tells us more about the subject or predicate.

Types of Phrases

There are four types of phrases. While I don't think it's necessary for you to memorize and define each type, I do think it's important for you to recognize a group of words acting as a phrase when you see one. I also think it's cool to begin thinking of the implications phrases can have on your writing. Phrases give you a way to add variety to your writing and to mix up the patterns of your sentences. (See Chapter Six for more details.)

1. The Prepositional Phrase

This is the most common type of phrase. It's a group of words starting with a preposition and ending with a noun or pronoun (known as the *object* of the preposition). There may be several other descriptive words in between the preposition and the noun or pronoun at the end, but at the very minimum the phrase must have at least two words.

Examples	under the table	to me
	with the large nose ring	after the operation

If you haven't already done so, I strongly urge you to memorize the list of common prepositions on page 28. I am not the kind of person who thinks there's much in the world important enough to memorize, but this does happen to be one place where I become the bespectacled, bun-in-the-hair English teacher. If you can point to a prepositional phrase in a sentence you immediately know something about the words in that phrase: the subject of the sentence is not in that phrase. Let me repeat:

The subject of a sentence is never, never, never in a prepositional phrase.

Trust me. It will become important later on that you can find the subject of a

Name _____   Date _____

sentence. Knowing you don't have to waste your time looking inside a prepositional phrase is helpful.

Here's another important thing you need to know about all phrases: Entire phrases can be used as a part of speech. Prepositional phrases can either be an **adjective** or **adverb**.

The prepositional phrase acting as an adjective:

The boys **in the band** played the kazoo. (Which boys?)

The dress **with the sequins** is blue. (What kind of dress?)

The prepositional phrase acting as an adverb:

He ran **down the alley** hoping to find an escape. (Where did he run?)

The boy sat **between his mother and father at the trial.**

(There are actually two phrases in that sentence. Where did he sit? When did he do it?)

One more thing about prepositional phrases: You can usually take them out of a sentence entirely and still have a complete sentence. All prepositional phrases do is add more information or description about the basic idea of the sentence.

Verbals

The next three types of phrases are classified as **verbals** because they start with some form of the verb. Big deal, you think. Actually, it is. In fact, when I learned about these, my writing changed. Fireworks exploded and whistles blew in my head because I found a way to start a sentence that looked like I was beginning with the predicate part even when I wasn't. (O.K., I'll tell you the truth, I didn't really realize what I was doing, I just knew my writing seemed to have more drama to it.) So, pay attention to these next three types of phrases. They are very cool.

2. The Gerund Phrase

Here's what happens. You take a verb, you add *-ing*, and presto—that verb becomes a noun. Watch.

Examples	**Voting on election day** is an important part of being a good citizen.
	(Can you see it? That gerund phrase is acting as the subject of the sentence, so therefore it must be a noun.)
	By voting on election day you become a good citizen.

(Now we have a gerund phrase with the gerund being used as the object of the preposition *by*, and since we know every prepositional phrase ends with a noun or pronoun, **voting** must be a noun. As a side note, some grammar types would call the entire phrase **By voting on election day** the gerund phrase, and you can, too, since it all flows together. Or, you can call it a gerund phrase connected to a prepositional phrase—you get to decide how picky you want to be.)

Doesn't it seem as if you're starting a sentence with the predicate? The *feel* of a

Name _____   Date _____

gerund is action and even if you're the only person who knows what you're doing, who cares? You've made your writing better, and that's what really counts.

3. The Infinitive Phrase

This phrase is made up of the word *to* plus a verb, and suddenly you've got two words acting like a **noun**, an **adjective**, or an **adverb**.

Examples	
	to pretend to play to go to think
	To learn English before returning to Burma is Aung's goal.
	(The infinitive phrase here is the subject of the sentence, so it's a noun.)
	Aung had the desire and the motivation **to learn English before returning to Burma**.
	(The infinitive phrase is describing the desire and motivation, so it's an adjective.)
	Aung studies **to learn**.
	(Why does Aung study? The infinitive phrase answers the verb's question, so it's an adverb.)

Usually, you will find the infinitive is used as a noun, but it is possible to use it as those other parts of speech. One thing you need to be careful about is being able to tell when the word "to" is an infinitive and when it's a preposition. Look at the following, and put parentheses around the infinitive phrase and then circle the prepositional phrase:

To go to the circus is fun.

4. The Participial Phrase

In Chapter 1 you saw that the participle is one of the basic parts of a verb. You can have a present participle, which is the verb plus *-ing*, or its past, which is usually the verb plus *-ed* or one of the gazillion exceptions ending in *-d, -t, -en,* or *-n*. When the participle is hooked up with other descriptive words to become a participial phrase, the entire phrase acts as an **adjective**. That's important to remember because sometimes when you see a verb ending in *-ing* you might assume it's a gerund, so you have to figure out if the phrase is acting as a noun or an adjective.

Examples	
	Shaking the dust behind him, Sherlock left Texas forever.
	(The phrase is telling us more about the noun Sherlock, so it's an adjective.)
	I found an old suitcase **filled with dirty clothing**.
	(Which suitcase? The one filled with dirty clothing—so once again we have a participial phrase describing the noun.)

Name _____   Date _____

Remember, it's not critical for you to memorize the types of phrases and then methodically plop them in your writing. I'm not sure it's even necessary to be able to tell how a phrase is being used or even which one is being used in any given sentence. (Unless, of course, you're one of those people who delights in knowing details.) What is important, however, is for you to begin to see phrases as friends that can improve your writing. The prepositional phrase is simply a way to add information to a sentence, but the verbals can put a whole new spin on a sentence. If you feel like your writing has no "pep" to it and every sentence has the same pattern, look at the verb in the sentence. See if you can begin the sentence with a verbal phrase to make it look like your sentence is starting with action. It's a sure-fire way to add some spice to whatever it is you're writing.

 *Exercise 2.2*

Directions: In the sentences below, underline each group of words acting as a phrase. Many sentences have more than one phrase. If you're feeling especially clever, see if you can explain what type of phrase each is, and how it is being used.

1. That book on the shelf in the center of the library is a classic.

2. The dog jumped over the fence, into the alley, and around the corner to avoid being caught by the dogcatcher.

3. Fighting a severe stomach flu, Louise went to school anyway so she wouldn't miss learning more about grammar.

4. To make the basketball team is Maggie's goal.

5. The student hoped to become a writer herself one day.

6. That child drawing all over the wall is my son.

7. Driving a car at 16 is perfectly legal in most states.

8. Ms. Cleveland, our inspirational speech teacher, is so dynamic that her classes actually can't wait to speak in front of large audiences.

9. Leaping to her feet, Zoe ran to the stage when the magician asked for a volunteer from the audience.

10. The waitress at the restaurant was so slow we began to wonder if our food would ever come.

 *Grammar, Mechanics, and Usage*

Name _____   Date _____

Clauses

Like phrases, clauses are groups of words that act together in a sentence. But the difference between phrases and clauses is great.

 A CLAUSE is a group of words that has a complete subject and a complete predicate.

There are two types of clauses:

1. **An Independent clause—This is just another name for a sentence. It's a group of words that has a subject and a predicate and expresses a complete thought.**

2. **A Dependent Or subordinating clause—This is a group of words that has a subject and a predicate, but cannot stand alone as a sentence.**

Independent clauses are just that—independent. They are groups of words that can stand alone. They need no further explanation since they're just a fancier way of defining what a sentence is.

Dependent or subordinating clauses need to be looked at more closely. As their name implies, they are groups of words that depend on something else (the rest of the sentence) to make sense. Look at the groups of words below. Both of them contain a subject (the noun or pronoun the sentence is written about) and a predicate (the verb and other words that tell us what the subject is or is doing). But can these groups of words stand alone?

If the rain ever stops.

When the fall comes.

Yes, there is a subject and a predicate, but these groups of words don't make sense by themselves. They need the rest of the sentence to complete the thought. Now look:

If the rain ever stops, I'll be able to work in my garden.

When the fall comes, it's apple-picking time.

Now we've got a group of words that makes sense. In each of the two examples above, we have a dependent and an independent clause working together to create one understandable sentence. But, in reality, who cares?

Actually, no one.

All anybody really wants you to know is, don't be fooled by everything you know. Just because a sentence has a noun or pronoun and a verb (a subject and a predicate) don't assume you've got a true sentence on your hands. You've got to be sure those words make sense or else you don't really have a sentence.

Name _____   Date _____

 *Exercise 2.3*

Directions: Just to show off, in the sentences below underline the independent clauses once and the dependent clauses twice.

1. My friend, who is Italian, is an excellent cook.

2. Because it looked like rain, the game was canceled.

3. I want to visit Ireland someday, since it's supposed to be a beautiful country.

4. My favorite book, which was written by Betty Smith, is *A Tree Grows in Brooklyn.*

5. Although skiing is an expensive hobby, the joy of schussing down the slopes outweighs the pain of forking over so much cash.

6. The family whose dog always roams the neighborhood lives on the corner.

7. The car that I like best is a Porsche.

8. When Peter is on the playground, he always makes new friends.

9. Wherever you visit in Germany, you are reminded of the effects of World War II.

10. Unless you've been through an exercise program, you have no idea how much your life can change when fitness becomes part of your everyday life.

    (There are actually two dependent clauses in this sentence.)

Chapter 3: Sentence Errors

Background Notes

This chapter confronts the four most common types of errors your students make when writing: fragments, run-ons, subject/verb agreement, and pronoun/antecedent agreement. It explains the problems and gives lots of exercises to help analyze them. However, remember our goal is to make sure our students can find their own errors, not ones from a drill book, so think of ways to bring their own work into this chapter.

Questions to Ask Students

What's the difference between oral and written language? Why is it O.K. to *speak* in fragments and run-ons, but not to write them? Should we correct people when they are speaking even if the dialect they are speaking doesn't need to have subject/verb agreement?

What to Do on Day One

Read the following sentences orally to the class. Add more of your own if you wish. Have the students number a piece of paper from 1–5. Tell them that if you read a correct sentence they should write a C by the number. If the sentence is incorrect for any reason they know of, they should write NC for not correct.

1. One of my CDs have disappeared. (NC—subject "one" does not agree with verb "have")
2. Some of the teachers live near the school. (C)
3. Every student who works up to their capacity will receive a passing grade. (NC—pronoun "their" does not agree with antecedent "student")
4. Neither performer was at his best. (C, but could be rewritten to avoid the masculine pronoun "he." E.g., The performers were not at their best.)
5. During the long drive to the wrestling meet in western California. (NC—fragment)

Use this exercise as a springboard to discuss how sometimes you can rely on your ear to help you detect grammatical errors, but sometimes you can't. Sometimes what sounds right isn't, and vice versa.

Especially for ESL

Undoubtedly, this whole idea of hearing what's right and what's not won't work for our ESL students. Assure these students, however, that the rules are pretty clear for these major sentence errors and that they will be able to figure out what's correct simply by analyzing each sentence they write.

(continued)

Chapter 3:
Sentence Errors *(continued)*

Extension Activities

Since it's often easy to find mistakes on another's worksheet, but not in our own work, we want to spend some time having students pick out their own mistakes. With student permission, show student compositions on an overhead. Have the class look for sentence errors together. While this might seem like courting disaster, I have never found a class longing to tear apart a fellow classmate's work. It also helps to tell students that throughout the year you will be making an overhead of at least one composition from every member of the class, so sooner or later everyone will get a turn. This technique also helps foster the peer editing we want in writing.

Chapter 3: Sentence Errors

If only we could say that knowing what a sentence is prevents sentence errors! Unfortunately, sometimes in the fever of writing we forget a few basics. If you remember that every sentence you write must be a group of words that makes sense and must have both a subject and a predicate, you'll be well on your way to never making any of these fatal errors. Let's see what the most common errors are and then let's get rid of them in our writing once and for all.

Fatal Error #1: Sentence Fragments

A fragment is a group of words pretending to be a sentence. Something is missing: either the subject or the predicate. It doesn't matter which. The point is, a sentence fragment is just a group of words that does not form a complete thought and so it can't be a sentence.

You do not want to write fragments; not once, not ever.

(Unless of course you become a published author . . . then you can do just about anything you want. More on that later.)

Writers sometimes try to pass off a dependent clause as a sentence. Here's the type of sentence that often tries to be passed off as complete:

While I sat on the subway.

When you look at it all by itself like that you can probably easily tell that yes, you do have a subject (I), and you even know what "I" did (sat on the subway). Although this fragment has a predicate, it's easy to see that this group of words just doesn't make sense by itself, right? You need to tack on an independent clause to "round out" the writer's intent. To fix it up, you need to add a comma and come up with a fitting conclusion to the thought. For example:

While I sat on the subway, I saw an old friend.

Now we have a complete subject and a complete predicate that together add up to a complete sentence. That's exactly what we want for every sentence.

Just to begin to tease you about punctuation, notice that in the sentence above there's a comma at the place where the independent clause connects to the dependent one. That's a basic comma rule, and now's as good a time as any to start paying attention to punctuation. Here's how the rule goes:

 If a sentence starts with a dependent clause that begins with a subordinating conjunction, you will need a comma at the place where the dependent clause connects to the independent one.

(Don't panic if the above seems like mumbo jumbo to you. You'll get it as we practice. I promise.)

Name _____ Date _____

Look what happens if I reverse the sentence:

I saw an old friend while I sat on the subway.

The most important thing is that the sentence is complete no matter which way I write it. But it's cool to have some choice about how you're going to get your ideas across and to let punctuation help you out. Look at another example of this idea:

Incomplete: After she left Rwanda.

Complete: After she left Rwanda, Hadiya went to a refugee camp in Liberia.

OR

Hadiya went to a refugee camp in Liberia after she left Rwanda.

Not every fragment starts with a subordinating conjunction. Sometimes writers just think any old group of words that starts with a capital and ends with a period will work as a sentence. Look:

Incomplete: That appeared during the middle of the storm.

(Again, there is a subject and a predicate, but it just doesn't hold together to express a complete thought, so some extra words are needed to finish the idea.)

Complete: The hailstones that appeared during the middle of the storm were as big as golf balls.

Incomplete: Swimming nearly 50 laps a day.

Complete: Swimming nearly 50 laps a day will build strong muscles.

Grammar, Mechanics, and Usage

Name _____   Date _____

Exercise 3.1

Directions: Now, take the following fragments and write full-fledged sentences on the lines provided. Try your best to show your knowledge of commas in each answer. If you want, write each sentence that has a subordinating conjunction in two ways.

1. Which seemed like the right thing to do at the time.

   _____

   _____

2. If you want to impress me.

   _____

   _____

3. Because he needed the money.

   _____

   _____

4. Speaks fluently in Spanish.

   _____

   _____

5. Since we were going his way.

   _____

   _____

The big problem with fragments generally occurs when you're just writing so quickly you forget to make sure every sentence is complete. Here's an example of what often happens:

During the holidays Uncle Frank came with gifts for the entire family. A wristwatch for me and a new computer game for my sister. We just loved it when he came. Because he was our favorite uncle. If he lived with us every day. I'm not sure we'd appreciate him as much as we do now. I sure hope he knows how special he is. To everyone in our family.

Even though the basic meaning of the paragraph is clear because the context makes sense of all the words, the paragraph above is filled with fragments and just doesn't work. Even if the ideas are clear in your mind, make sure you're not writing fragments all over the place.

Use your pencil and fix up that paragraph above about Uncle Frank. You may need to add words or marks of punctuation. Make sure every sentence is complete. Do not depend only on the context of the words to make sense of the paragraph.

Grammar, Mechanics, and Usage

Name _____ Date _____

 Exercise 3.2

Directions: Another common error with fragments often occurs with the verb. Again, because that brain of yours is quicker than your pen (or keyboard), it's easy to leave out part of the verb. Add what is needed to the sentences below. HINT: Look at the verb!

1. Steffi Graf winning the tennis match.

2. My friends gone to a dude ranch.

3. Steve's letter published in *The Miami Herald*.

4. For two years Joan working as a word processor.

5. You ever been to San Francisco?

Name _____ Date _____

Fatal Error #2: Run-Ons

The name says it all. These are sentences that just go on and on and on. Here the writer again forgets the definition of a sentence. Instead he or she just keeps stringing subjects and predicates together without ever stopping to look at what's being created. Usually one of two mistakes occurs here:

1. The writer keeps adding the word "and" to join thoughts together.

   OR

2. The writer just puts commas everywhere to string ideas together.

   Here's an example:

   Herb talks too much, nobody seems to mind.

   There are two complete ideas here:

1. Herb talks too much.

2. Nobody seems to mind.

   To correct it you can do one of three things:

1. Write two separate sentences.

   Herb talks too much. Nobody seems to mind.

2. Use a comma and a conjunction.

   Herb talks too much, but nobody seems to mind.

3. Connect the two using a semicolon.

   Herb talks too much; nobody seems to mind.

NOTE: In the next chapter we'll go into great detail about the use of the semicolon. You should be forewarned, however, that I think this is a mark of punctuation to use sparingly.

Grammar, Mechanics, and Usage

Name _____   Date _____

Exercise 3.3

Directions: Correct the run-ons in the following paragraph. You may need to add or delete words and punctuation.

My favorite childhood vacations were the trips my family took to the beach each year I just loved being the first of my brothers and sisters to run into the water and begin jumping the waves. Even after repeated warnings from my mother, I just couldn't contain my excitement, and so I would run out into the frigid waters and before I knew it I was way out to sea then I would hear my mother's voice. Usually I had drifted far away from my family's blanket and I could tell from the nervous sound in my mother's voice that I had scared her, and then when I'd finally get back to her she'd tell me to please try and pay more attention to where I was going but it didn't take long before I'd be way out in the deep waters again. Eventually she'd give in and insist on jumping waves with me I think it was the only way she could be sure to know where I was. To this day, the sound of the waves makes me want to hold my mother's hand.

Grammar, Mechanics, and Usage

Name _____   Date _____

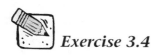 *Exercise 3.4*

Directions: Let's see if you can identify and correct both fragments and run-ons when you see them. The following paragraph has a number of sentence mistakes. Underline any fragments. Circle any run-ons. Leave complete sentences as they are. Then rewrite the paragraph correctly on the lines provided. Feel free to add little words to connect thoughts, but try not to totally change the meaning of the paragraph.

It is often difficult to recognize fragments and run-ons in paragraphs. Because the sentences are close together and seem to make sense. Most writers just assume their readers know what they mean, they just keep on writing as if they were talking. It really helps to look at one sentence at a time you can see the problems then. If you're careful. How does it seem so far? Let's put a couple more sentences together and see if it is still making sense to you. You need to remember it's not the length of the sentence that matters or the placement of punctuation it's whether the sentence has a subject and a predicate, and expresses a complete thought. As you write more and more sentences. You will see the difference in your writing. The important thing is to keep checking your work. Writing isn't easy, there's a good feeling you get when you know you've expressed your ideas clearly.

_____

_____

_____

_____

_____

_____

_____

_____

_____

_____

_____

_____

_____

Grammar, Mechanics, and Usage

Name _____ Date _____

Fatal Error #3: Problems with Subject/Verb Agreement

A subject/verb agreement mistake is a slightly more difficult problem than the first two we looked at. You have to identify the subject and verb in every sentence you write. Usually this is no problem since your ear will tell you what's right just by the sound of the sentence. However, occasionally there are times you can't trust what you hear. Let's make sure you understand the basic theory.

When you and a friend agree on something, the two of you have matching ideas or beliefs. The key is that you *match*. The same thing is true for this grammatical issue: You must be sure your subject matches your verb. The basic rule is this:

 Singular subjects take singular verbs, and plural subjects take plural verbs.

Example	**The light flickers.** (singular subject, singular verb)
	The lights flicker. (plural subject, plural verb)

Easy enough, right?

The key is to find your subject, decide whether it's singular or plural, and plug in the right verb. A helpful hint to remember is that when third-person-singular subjects (he, she, it) need a present-tense verb, the verb will end in *-s*: he feels, she describes, it hovers. "I" and the singular "you" don't end in *-s*: I feel, you describe. Most verbs not ending in *-s* (are, were, have) are plural: they are, they count, they feel.

If this all sounds too complicated for you, don't worry. If you've been speaking English all your life you probably already know this and your ear will tell you what sounds right. If English is still new to you, remember you're still practicing and your "ear" just needs time to get adjusted to this new language. However, no matter how long you've been using the language there are some sentences that simply require more thinking. We'll review some of the bigger subject/verb agreement issues.

Agreement Issue #1—When a prepositional phrase comes between a subject and a verb, the verb must agree with the subject. Remember the mantra? *The subject of a sentence is never, never, never in a prepositional phrase.* Don't be fooled into thinking the object of the preposition is the subject of the sentence.

Example	**The chairs on the porch are painted white.**
	Subject = chairs
	Chairs = plural subject
	Are = plural verb

Agreement Issue #2—The following indefinite pronouns are considered singular:

anyone anybody each either

Grammar, Mechanics, and Usage

Name _____   Date _____

| | every | everybody | everyone | neither |
| | no one | one | someone | somebody |

If one of these pronouns is the subject of a sentence, make sure you have a singular verb.

Example	**Everybody wishes for more money.** (Think of it as every *single* body.) ***Each* of the boys *wishes* for more money.** (Each *one* of the boys.) ***Neither* of them *has* enough money.** (Neither *one* of those people has enough cash.) ***Somebody has* to save that dog from drowning!** (Here we're hoping that *one* person will be brave enough to save the dog.)

Agreement Issue #3—Conversely, the following indefinite pronouns are considered plural:

| | several | few | both | many |

Example	**Few of my family understand me.** (Plural subject "few" requires plural verb "understand.") **Both of your excuses sound reasonable.** ("Both" is the subject here because "excuses" is in a prepositional phrase, and since "both" is plural, you need the plural verb "sound.")

Grammar, Mechanics, and Usage

Name _____ Date _____

Exercise 3.5

Directions: Do the following on your own to see if these rules are sinking in. First, circle the subject, then circle the correct verb in each sentence.

1. The houses in that neighborhood (*cost, costs*) too much.

2. The cause of many illnesses (*is, are*) poor diet.

3. Everybody in our family (*are, is*) planning a trip this summer.

4. Many of us (*like, likes*) long books.

5. Cells in your brain (*need, needs*) oxygen.

6. Somebody in the audience (*was, were*) snoring.

7. His lack of knowledge (*amaze, amazes*) me.

8. Both of my parents (*has, have*) red hair.

9. They (*was, were*) expecting us to visit them last summer.

10. One American in 10 (*drink, drinks*) too much.

    Great! You're getting this, I'm sure. So let's go on and look at some of the other complicating rules.

Agreement Issue #4—Watch out for sentences starting with *there* or *here*. "There" or "here" is never the subject of the sentence, so be on the lookout for the subject somewhere after the verb.

Examples	**Here are the papers you ordered.** (The subject is *papers* because that's what the sentence is talking about; it requires the plural verb "are.") **There has been trouble here.** (The subject is *trouble*, so it uses the singular verb "has been.")

Agreement Issue #5—Be careful with questions, too. The subject will follow the verb in these sentences as well.

Examples	**Why are they singing?** (Turn the question into a statement to find the subject. So this becomes: **They** are singing, why?) (Now you can see that "they" is the subject, and since the subject is plural you need a plural verb, "are singing.") **Where is Bob?** (This becomes: **Bob** is where? Now it's easy to see that Bob is the subject, and since he's just one guy, you need that singular verb, "is.")

Name _____ Date _____

Agreement Issue #6—Subjects joined by *and* take a plural verb. Subjects joined by *or* or *nor* take a singular verb.

Examples	**Mother and Aunt Sue left for Canada.** (This sentence is about two people, Mother and Aunt Sue, so we need a plural verb.) **Either Mother or Aunt Sue is sure to know the way.** (Either *one* of them knows the way, so we need the singular verb "is.") **Neither Mother nor Aunt Sue has ever been to Canada before.** (Even though there are two different people in this sentence, we are thinking of them as individuals, so we need the singular verb "has been.")

Agreement Issue #7—Every once in a while you have to sit back and consider the meaning of the entire sentence to determine whether the subject is plural or singular. Sometimes collective nouns are considered as one unit, sometimes not. Likewise, the indefinite pronouns *some, any, none, all,* and *most* can be either singular or plural.

Examples	**Some** of the movie **was** exciting. ("Some" stands for a part of, so it takes a singular verb, "was.") **Some** of my friends **are going** to the dance, but I'm staying home. ("Some" stands for *many*, so it takes a plural verb, "are going.")

Agreement Issue #8—When the subject of a sentence is a space of time, a sum of money, a measurement, weight, volume, or fraction, you usually use a singular verb.

Examples	**Four years** in a foreign country **seems** like a long time. (We're thinking of the years as one unit of time, so we use a singular verb.) These **last four years have been filled** with adventure. (Now we're thinking of each individual year, so we need the plural verb.) **One half** of the class **was** absent. (The singular verb is used because the subject is thought of as a unit.) **Seven dollars** is enough to cover the cost of the movie. (Even though it's seven individual bills, we're thinking of it as one lump sum of money, so the subject is singular and takes the singular verb "is.")

If some of these issues are beginning to sound picky, try not to think too much about them. Trust yourself. Most likely the answer that *sounds* right, is.

Grammar, Mechanics, and Usage

Name _____ Date _____

Exercise 3.6

Directions: In the following sentences, first circle the subject and decide whether you need a singular or plural verb. Then, circle the correct verb.

1. Sam and his brothers (*sleep, sleeps*) in this tent.

2. The estate, including the paintings, (*was, were*) sold.

3. Either Friday or Saturday (*appear, appears*) to be the best time to meet for coffee.

4. The fruit at the farmer's market (*look, looks*) tempting.

5. Fifteen dollars (*is, are*) not enough to buy a pair of Nikes™.

6. All of my free time (*is, are*) spent in the kitchen.

7. That team (*has, have*) won the Super Bowl three times.

8. Two weeks (*is, are*) not enough time for a trip abroad.

9. Barbara and the others in her dormitory (*sleep, sleeps*) late on Saturdays.

10. Neither the CEO of the firm nor the sales manager (*is, are*) a college graduate.

11. Three fourths of the graduating seniors (*plan, plans*) to further their education.

12. A few of the actors (*hope, hopes*) to become directors one day.

13. Neither Yuri nor Svetlana (*earn, earns*) enough money to make a down payment on a new car.

14. Max and his cousins (*celebrate, celebrates*) Passover at their grandmother's house.

15. Thea or Kendra (*is, are*) going to buy the store one day.

Grammar, Mechanics, and Usage

Name _____ Date _____

Fatal Error #4: Problems with Pronoun/Antecedent Agreement

Let's refresh your memory on the basics of pronouns:

1. A pronoun must agree with its antecedent in **person** (the first-person pronoun is *I*, the second is *you*, the third is *he, she, it;* and *we, you,* and *they* are the plurals); **number** (singular or plural); and **gender** (masculine, feminine, or neuter sex). You don't always need to have all three to have agreement, but you must have at least two of the three requirements.

And

2. You need to learn the case forms of pronouns and how they are used in the sentence.

Well, the time has come to make sure this is not all gibberish to you. Let's tackle that first issue head-on.

You remember that an antecedent is the noun a pronoun refers to or is replacing. It usually is a noun that comes before the pronoun.

Example	**Jodd** loved **his** Corvette. ("Jodd" is the antecedent for "his.")

Though this seems like a rather simple sentence, there are actually a few things going on. That pronoun "his" *matches* or *agrees with* its antecedent in three ways:

1. Person—The word "Jodd" needs a third-person pronoun to refer to it, and that's exactly what "his" is. In fact, to be specific, it's a third-person, possessive-case pronoun.

2. Number—"Jodd" is singular and the pronoun "his" is singular.

3. Gender—"Jodd" is male and "his" is the male pronoun.

Here's another example:

Karine left **her** purse at the restaurant.

"Her" is the correct pronoun to use because we need a third-person pronoun to refer to Karine. "Her" is also singular and indicates a female gender, all of which are necessary for this simple little sentence.

Obviously, it doesn't take a rocket scientist to figure out these examples. So let's take a look at where the problems come in. What's the antecedent for "their" in the following sentence?

Ali and **Shir** sold **their** much-loved Indian restaurant to a competitor.

Ali and *Shir* are the antecedents for the pronoun "their." We chose "their" because it is the third-person-plural pronoun, and that's two of the requirements we needed to fulfill. The thing is, "their" does not reflect gender. We can't tell from the pronoun "their" whether Ali and Shir are men or women. If you're from India or Pakistan you'd have no trouble recognizing these names as masculine, but an English speaker might run into some difficulties.

But the real problem with this issue comes up when the antecedent for a

Grammar, Mechanics, and Usage

Name _____   Date _____

pronoun is one of the indefinite pronouns—*each, every, any*, etc. (see page 7 for a complete list of the indefinite pronouns). Believe it or not, this problem has caused national debate. I bet you didn't think anything English teachers did would be of global concern, but guess again.

Here's what's at issue. Sometimes we have no way of knowing what gender the subject is, and it would be incorrect to use a plural pronoun when a singular one is needed. So, we've invented all sorts of clever ways around this. Look at this sentence:

Each student should bring his notebook to class every day.

The antecedent for *his* is "each student." We know that's singular and we need a third-person pronoun, but we don't know the gender of the student. It's clearly incorrect to write this sentence, "**Each** student should bring **their** notebook to class every day," because the sentence must have a singular pronoun to refer to the singular antecedent "each." Our answer to this

problem for the first thousand years English was being recorded was to just put everything into the masculine gender as we did above. However, as the feminist movement began to take hold, our language tried to reflect our politics and show equality. So we came up with the following as a way to avoid the problem:

Each student should bring his or her notebook to class every day.

Guess what? That didn't work either. It's just too cumbersome to keep filling in both the feminine and masculine form of the pronoun. Then too, it became an issue about which pronoun should go first: should it be *his or her* or *her or his*? You've probably read texts where the author starts

out with a disclaimer and sometimes even goes so far as to flip gender and position in each chapter. Well, we Americans are just too lazy, and so you'll probably notice this usage is on its way out.

Here's what to do:

Avoid the problem entirely by simply rewriting any sentence that presents this problem.

Don't play the game and you'll always win. Watch how we can rewrite that troublesome sentence:

All students should bring their notebooks to class each day.

The meaning of the sentence is essentially the same, and we don't get anybody mad at us. Let's look at more examples:

Troublesome: Everyone feels discouraged at some time in his school career.

Avoiding the problem: Most students feel discouraged at some time in their school career.

Troublesome: Neither of the musicians remembered to bring his music stand to the concert.

Better: Both musicians forgot to bring their music stand to the concert.

Troublesome: Each of our friends will visit her favorite national park this summer.

Better: All of our friends will visit their favorite national park this summer.

Grammar, Mechanics, and Usage

Name _____ Date _____

 *Exercise 3.7*

Directions: Let's practice. First look for the antecedent of the pronoun and underline it. Then circle the correct pronoun in each sentence. If you encounter any gender problems, rewrite the sentence to avoid them.

1. Neither of the girls had brought (*her, their*) skis along on the vacation.

2. Mrs. James was angry because several of the students left (*his, their*) homework at home.

3. Because it was "find another way to work day," nobody drove (*his, their*) car.

4. The officers meet every third Thursday at a local restaurant for (*his, their*) monthly business meeting.

5. If anyone knows the best way to do this math problem, (*he, they*) should tell me.

Now let's go headlong into that second issue: case forms of pronouns and how they are used in a sentence.

You need to learn the case forms of pronouns and how they are used in a sentence.

The personal pronouns fall into three "cases," or categories: nominative, objective, and possessive. We've already discussed these in Chapter One, but let's review the two that cause the most problems.

The Nominative-Case Pronouns

I   he   she   we   they

These five pronouns should be used only if they are acting as either the subject of a sentence or as a predicate pronoun. In other words, the pronoun has to be either what the sentence is about (the subject) or it has to appear in the predicate part of the sentence following a *linking verb*.

Pronoun as subject of sentence: She and **I** are good friends.

Pronoun as predicate pronoun: It was **they** at the hot dog stand.

(I know that doesn't look right, but technically it is. You can check it yourself by turning the sentence around a bit: They were at the hot dog stand.)

The Objective-Case Pronouns

me   him   her   us   them

If you find a pronoun acting as a direct object, an indirect object, or the object of a preposition (hence objective case), you must use one of these five pronouns:

Pronoun as direct object: I told **him**.

Grammar, Mechanics, and Usage

Name _____   Date _____

Here we have a pronoun in the predicate part of a sentence following an action verb. Direct objects answer the question *who* or *what* after an action verb.

Pronoun as indirect object: I told **him** the news.

Again, there's a pronoun in the predicate following an action verb. So I get this by first finding the direct object: I told what? The news. Then I find the indirect object by asking *to whom?* or *for whom?* To whom did I tell the news? To him.

NOTE: Be careful! Sometimes you can have a sentence that appears to have an action verb with a pronoun in the predicate, but you don't use these objective pronouns. Look at this example:

| **Example** | I wish he liked me. |

What you really have here are two independent clauses: *I wish* and *he liked me.* So I need a subject for my second clause. That's why *he* is correct, not *him.*

Pronoun as object of the preposition: The umpire stood between **us.**

(Here's another reason why it's good to memorize all those prepositions. Whenever you see one, you know a noun or pronoun has to be at the end of the phrase, and so you'd have to use an objective case pronoun.)

A Few More Glitches ...

When a pronoun is used with a noun (we girls, us girls) you can figure out which pronoun to use by getting rid of the noun and seeing how the pronoun is used in the sentence.

| **Example** | They blame (us, we) girls for everything. (Do they blame *us* or *we* for everything? Obviously it's **us!** |

When a pronoun is helping to make a comparison (usually following the words *like* or *as*), complete the comparison mentally by adding in the left-out words. Then assess how the pronoun is being used.

| **Examples** | Ferdinand is taller than (I, me). (We're really saying, "Ferdinand is taller than **I** *am.*") |
| | The guidelines help you as much as (I, me). ("The guidelines help you as much as *they help* **me.**") |

Be careful—occasionally the whole meaning of the sentence can change if you alter it too much.

Diana likes Tom more than I (more than I like him).

OR

Diana likes Tom more than me (more than she likes me).

Again, don't think too much. Often your ear will help you out.

Grammar, Mechanics, and Usage

Name _____   Date _____

One last note: In the great who/whom debate, you should know that *who* is considered a nominative-case pronoun and *whom* is in the objective case. Personally, I think this is yet another example of our spoken language having a jump on our written language. I predict that in 100 years, no one will be using *whom*. Until then, follow the rules as you know them, but you're usually safe just using *who* if you're totally confused.

Exercise 3.8

Directions: In the following sentences, circle the correct pronoun. Whenever possible, underline the antecedent, and tell how the pronoun is being used in the sentence. For a few of the sentences it is a good idea to totally rewrite them to avoid gender issues.

1. Reba exercises more often than (*I, me*).

2. For (*us, we*) there is nothing like a glass of refreshing lemonade on a hot day.

3. (*We, Us*) women deserve equal pay for equal work.

4. Everyone in the group hoped (*his, their*) number would win.

5. Why don't you give (*we, us*) short people a chance to play basketball?

6. If you see anybody I know, tell (*him, them*) hello for me.

7. If it were up to Angelo and (*she, her*), they would spend all their time searching for out-of-print books.

8. Usually Ronald is more careful than (*I, me*).

9. That was probably Horatio and (*they, them*) at the back door.

10. If anyone had ever seen a glacier (*she, they*) wouldn't be able to forget it.

11. After a person retires, (*they, he*) often moves down south.

12. Each of the jurors has made up (*her, their*) mind.

13. Many of the hikers wore (*his, their*) fleece cover-ups.

14. Will Dominic or (*he, him*) bring the keys to the shop?

15. My supervisor took Pete and (*I, me*) out to lunch.

Grammar, Mechanics, and Usage

Chapter 4: Punctuation

Background Notes

Punctuation is the "body language" of writing. It is the written equivalent of facial expressions and gestures—visual cues for getting our point across. Punctuation provides rhythm to our words and often shows our reader how the words should be interpreted. It gives subliminal power to what we're writing. A firm grasp of the rules of punctuation can help your students add emphasis to what they're saying.

What to Do on Day One

Ask your class to name every mark of punctuation they've ever heard of. On the board draw several lines, duplicating the lines from a notebook page. Put the marks of punctuation they are shouting on the appropriate place on each line. For example, put a period at the end of one line and a semicolon somewhere in the middle. On another line, put a quotation mark at either end, with a comma in the middle. On a third line, put a question mark at the end, and so on. When you feel you've got them all, talk to your class about the visual effects of these marks. Two of the three end marks of punctuation (the exclamation point and the question mark) are a visual barrier for the eye. They say, "Stop right here a minute!" The comma's placement on the line reflects what it does in a sentence. We sort of trip over it and pause, which is exactly what we're supposed to do. The colon and the semicolon are, again, more visual road blocks forcing us to stop and pay

attention to what's on the other side of them. I use this friendly approach to punctuation because this is one of those places where students feel most at a loss. They're usually pretty clear on end marks, but everything else is up for grabs, so get them settled in with an art teacher's visual approach to what these marks are supposed to do to our eyes.

Extension Activities

Before you give out any of the student pages, write on the board some of the example sentences found in the text and have students go to the board to see if they can insert the necessary punctuation. This way you can find out exactly what it is they need to review in this chapter and use only those sections you feel your students need. I often also use quick daily dictation exercises as another way to do a fast hit on punctuation rules.

The thing about punctuation (and most issues in grammar) is that the rules and examples always seem so much simpler and clearer in a workbook than they do in students' own work. Since you want them to be able to apply the rules they're learning to their own writing, have students write their own sentences illustrating rules. Require a separate sentence for each of the comma rules. In this same vein, keep track of actual student mistakes from compositions they have turned in. Now you can either use their own work as a full class exercise, or you can come up with a worksheet of student-gener-

(continued)

Chapter 4:
Punctuation *(continued)*

ated examples that will have real meaning to them.

Outside Class Projects for Students

This chapter is my favorite opportunity for urging students to go out into their community to become the "grammar police." I give students extra points if they report back to the class on a mistake they saw on some restaurant menu. I excuse them from homework for a day if they are bold enough to speak to the store manager/owner about the problem. On a smaller scale, you can just have students bring in

mistakes from the newspaper or from a magazine article to share with the whole class.

It always amazes me how many businesses make glaring mistakes for the whole world to see in their advertising. This is a good place for students to listen to your own little version of "The Demise of the English Language and Why We Need to Preserve It." Maybe students could work up a speech of their own to present to a local business that they could first present to the class for extra credit.

Chapter 4: Punctuation

If you can figure out the basic rules and usages of punctuation, you can really improve your writing. Proper use of punctuation either enhances what it is you're saying or it detracts from it. When I learned about the power of the semicolon, it literally revolutionized my writing. So, sit back and enjoy the ride on this one. There's nothing that can happen here except making the writing you do even better.

End Marks

There are only three ways to end a sentence. Only three.
Either you use a period (.), a question mark (?), or an exclamation point (!).

 Periods indicate the end of a statement of fact or a sentence of command. They are also used in abbreviations and initials to indicate that you are not writing out the entire word.

Examples	It won't take long before you become a master of punctuation.
	Don't be cruel.
	Mr. Johnson was once the president. ("Mr." is an abbreviation of "Mister.")
	L.B. Johnson was once the president. ("L.B." is an abbreviation of the name "Lyndon Baines.")

NOTE: Several styles of abbreviations are often acceptable, some of which do not require a period; for example, AM or a.m.

 Question marks are used only after you've asked a direct question.

Examples	Oh where, oh where has my little dog gone?
	Why did you get your hair cut?

Name _____   Date _____

 Exclamation points are used at the end of sentences that express sudden emotion or feeling, or forceful commands. As a general rule your words should convey the feelings—not your punctuation. Reserve exclamation points for truly important statements.

Examples	Man overboard!
	Oh, no! Not another tattoo!

 *Exercise 4.1*

Directions: Punctuate the following:

1. She did not like living among the lizards and rattlesnakes

2. How wonderful it must be to grow up on a warm, sunny island

3. Oh my goodness Did you see the new teacher

4. What a great party this is

5. Did I ever tell you my middle name

Grammar, Mechanics, and Usage

Name _____   Date _____

Commas

Hooray! The moment you've waited for is here! Today you're finally going to figure out those little squiggles that have plagued you for years. O.K., maybe it won't all happen in one day, but the point is that the rules aren't really hard, and we do cut you some slack with commas. There's a thing called "poetic license," which basically means when you're the writer you can do whatever you want if it conveys your mean-ing. Most likely you've relied on the old "put a comma in wherever you pause" rule. Often that will work, especially when you're writing fiction. Read over the following as guidelines to comma usage, and try really hard not to get yourself all worked up over this.

Here are the two most important things you need to know about commas:

People either use them

1. everywhere

    OR

2. nowhere.

Before we go any further, decide which camp you're in. Now, look at the two statements below and put a check mark next to the one that most frequently goes through your head:

"I think this sentence needs a comma, so it probably doesn't."

OR

"I think this sentence doesn't need a comma, so it probably does."

Once you figure out where you stand on these two burning issues, you can really begin to learn about commas. For some reason commas seem to be a confidence test for most students. Trust your gut. We're going to review and practice with the most important comma rules to help build your confidence, not to frustrate you. So approach these rules as suggestions for comma usage and remember that as the writer you usually get to make the final call. Also, if you find the rules make no sense to you, concentrate on the examples. Usually the examples clearly show what the jumble of words can't.

Grammar, Mechanics, and Usage

Name _____ Date _____

The Only Comma Rules You Really Need to Know

1. The Series Rule

When you are listing a few things in a row (usually it's a list of nouns), separate each item with a comma. Commas should also be placed between two or more adjectives preceding a noun.

Example	Dylan likes jazz, rock, and blues. Marcella makes to-die-for meatballs, exquisite sauce, and perfect pasta.

Notice the circle around the last comma? That's because you can leave it in or take it out. Writer's choice. Just be consistent.

Examples of Adjectives Preceding a Noun:

She is a pretty, charming, kind young woman. (*Young woman* is a two-word noun here, thus there is no comma between *kind* and *young*.)

This rule does not apply if the two adjectives are thought of as one word, or if an adjective modifies the next adjective after it, and not the noun. (These are two ways of saying the same thing.)

Her dark red hair is beautiful.

2. Rule for Joining Two Sentences

When what you're really doing is combining two independent sentences into one longer sentence, and you use the conjunctions *and, but, or, nor, yet, so,* or *for,* put a comma BEFORE the conjunction.

Once again: The comma goes BEFORE the conjunction. Not on both sides of it, not after it, but BEFORE it!

Examples	*(conjunction in italics):* Sonya wants to go rollerblading, *but* I want to listen to a CD. He has access to the Internet, *and* now he's hoping to create his own web site. Lydia knew she loved Nigel, *yet* she wasn't sure she could actually marry him.

NOTE: In all of these examples I could have put a period where the comma is now. Then I would have omitted the conjunction, capitalized the first word of the next main clause, and I would have had two complete sentences. That would have been totally fine. Sometimes it's good to have short sentences, but sometimes it's not. This rule helps to give variety to your writing by showing you how to use coordinating conjunctions to create longer sentences. (See page 27 for more on conjunctions.)

Something to Think About: Why is no comma needed in the following?

He has access to the Internet and is hoping to create his own Web site.

Grammar, Mechanics, and Usage

Name _____ Date _____

Something Else to Think About: Please note, I did not say put a comma every time you use the word *and, but, or, nor,* etc. That's NOT what this rule says. Only if you have two complete sentences joined by a conjunction do you need the comma BEFORE the conjunction. However, if the two sentences are short, you don't need to use the comma.

Example	He is tired but he is happy.

 Exercise 4.2

Directions: Practice the first two comma rules on the sentences below. Put commas in wherever you think they are needed. Some sentences are fine the way they are and do not need a comma.

1. It's often a great deal of work but the holidays are usually worth the effort.
2. The signal was given the control button was pressed and the rocket burst into the sky on its first mission.
3. I never expected to see them again but like bad pennies they returned the next day.
4. Alex craned his neck and heard the scary noise again.
5. Proper equipment is needed for sailing across the Atlantic and an experienced crew is helpful.
6. The waiter brought a vegetarian omelet hash browns toast and coffee for breakfast.
7. She woke up and tried to fall back to sleep.
8. Hank went shopping and for once he didn't buy anything.
9. I met her on Monday and married her on Saturday.
10. It was a cold raw dark November day but I loved it.

3. Rule for Sentences Beginning with a Subordinating Conjunction or Introductory Clause

If a sentence begins with a subordinating conjunction (e.g., *although, because, while, until,* etc.), put a comma at the end of the dependent clause. If the subordinating conjunction is in the middle of the sentence, the comma is left out.

Or if you can hear it better this way...

When a sentence begins with an incomplete thought, join it to the rest of the sentence with a comma at the place it links with the real sentence.

However, when the incomplete thought is in the middle of the sentence, the comma is often not needed.

This rule tests whether you understand the difference between phrases and clauses, and can recognize a subordinating conjunction when you see one. Refer to page 27 on conjunctions and pages 38–44 on phrases and clauses. Look at the following examples, and I bet this will all make sense.

Name _____ Date _____

Examples	Although I don't want to admit it, commas are starting to make sense. **And Its Reverse** Commas are starting to make sense although I don't want to admit it. *Now read the rule over again. Does it make sense? Let's look at more examples:* Because I want to be a rock climber, I need to get the right kind of shoes. **And Its Reverse** I need to get the right kind of shoes because I want to be a rock climber.

Not all introductory clauses and phrases start with a subordinating conjunction. As long as the introductory clause is not acting as the subject of the sentence, it usually will take a comma.

Examples	Holding the torch in her hand, the athlete led the procession into the Olympic stadium. (Here we need the comma because the introductory phrase is just giving us additional information about that athlete.) *But if I rewrite the sentence this way, no comma is needed:* To carry the torch into the Olympic stadium is every athlete's dream. (Here the introductory phrase is acting as the subject of the sentence. It's essential to the meaning of the sentence and therefore no comma is needed.)

Something to Think About: If a sentence starts with several prepositional phrases, a comma comes after the last phrase.

Example	At the edge of the deep woods in the forests of rural Maine, he built a cabin.

4. Commas with Dialogue and Quotation Marks

This rule is simple: The comma goes INSIDE quotation marks. Always. No exceptions. Whether the quotation marks signify dialogue or anything else, the comma goes INSIDE. (The same rule applies to periods, by the way.)

Grammar, Mechanics, and Usage

Name _____ Date _____

If the dialogue is broken up by an interrupter, don't forget to add a comma after the interrupter.

Examples	"You'll be tested on every mark of punctuation you've ever heard of on Friday," the teacher snapped.
	AND
	"You'll be tested on every mark of punctuation you've ever heard of," the teacher snapped, "and Friday's the day."
	(Notice: I didn't have to capitalize the "A" in "and" because it's just a continuation of the sentence. You only have to capitalize after an interrupter if a new sentence is beginning.)
	AND
	Terry, known to the class as the "grammar king," passed the test with flying colors.

5. Words Not Really Essential to a Sentence

If there are words in a sentence that can be removed without changing the basic meaning of the sentence, you need commas around the words you could omit.

Examples	Mr. Wade, *the oldest man on the tour,* was the life of the party.
	(This sentence is really about Mr. Wade's high jinks. The fact that he's the oldest man on the tour is just extra information and not really necessary to the intent of the sentence.)
	My uncle, *who used to be a police officer,* now spends all his time on the golf course.
	(Italicized words are not necessary for a complete sentence.)
	Nicki, *I bet,* will go to the next Whitney Houston concert no matter where it is.
	(Italicized words are the speaker's interjection; without it, the thought is still complete.)
	Yes, I do hope to win the lottery one day.
	(The basic information here is that the writer wants free cash. The word "Yes" just tells us that the writer is responding to someone's question. It could be removed from the sentence and we'd still understand the statement.)

Name _____   Date _____

6. Dates and Addresses

Use commas to separate the city or town from the state, items in an address when they're written on a single line, day of the month from the year, day of the week from the day of the month and year, and items in a date when written in a sentence.

Examples	I once lived in Chicago, Illinois. Forward our mail to 10 Pleasant Street, Chicago, Illinois, beginning immediately. Bob's birth date is May 17, 1975. Bob's birth date is Monday, May 17, 1975. Bob was born on Monday, May 17, 1975, in East Meadow, New York.

 *Exercise 4.3*

Directions: In the following sentences, place commas where they are needed. Not all sentences require one.

1. While Ashley was talking to Kevin Jenna entered the room.

2. The quiet seaside soothed him into the relaxed state he needed for a vacation.

3. Some of the students were eating others were doing homework but most were just goofing off.

4. The girls had just enough money to buy their school supplies at the department store.

5. Having sailed around the world twice already Barney was looking for a new adventure.

6. When Kasia arrived from Poland she found learning a new language and the new cultural rules overwhelming.

7. Kyle asked "Maggie will you go with me to the movie on Saturday?"

8. The poet e.e. cummings did not use capital letters and his punctuation was frequently unconventional.

9. A child playing in the street risks losing his life.

10. Melanie moved to Richmond Virginia on June 1 1997 and in 1998 she plans to move to Dallas Texas.

11. Rock climbing has become a popular sport and its popularity seems to be growing.

12. Behaving like a spoiled child Frederick sulked until Edna gave in.

13. Sally's brother thought they should get two turkeys for Thanksgiving since 28 guests were planning to come.

Grammar, Mechanics, and Usage

Name _____   Date _____

14. I like chicken mayonnaise and mustard on my sandwich.

15. The two friendly students both got jobs at the gym.

16. Hagos will I am sure let me borrow the car tomorrow.

17. While taking an afternoon stroll in the park my little brother made friends with three squirrels two elderly gentlemen and a score of toddlers.

18. She is beautiful in fact stunning is more the word.

19. Peter's most prized possession was his 18-speed mountain bike.

20. "I began running at the age of 10" Aimee said "but I got serious about training in high school."

21. To drive across the country was Sophia's last wish.

22. Frank got a job at the Hotel Continental 443 Newbury Street Boston Massachusetts for the summer.

23. Blanca will help us after she finishes her own assignment.

24. Lisa one of my closest friends recently moved out of town.

25. Harriet was quite a talented ballplayer and made sure everyone knew it.

26. For breakfast we had ham and eggs orange juice toast and coffee.

27. My new friend Thung is hoping to find a job as an engineer which is what she was in Cambodia.

28. He thought the remark his wife made was either brilliant or the beginnings of a serious mental illness.

29. As we sat on the veranda of our spacious summer home we wondered how we would ever leave the place.

30. "Yes I'm talking to you" the angry mother informed her young son.

Name _____ Date _____

Apostrophes—Contractions and Possession

Let's get it straight from the very beginning:

You DO NOT use an apostrophe every time you write the letter "s."

Having said that, let's look at what the apostrophe does.

There are two major reasons to use an apostrophe. Either you want to do what we Americans do best—talk fast even in our writing—or you want to indicate possession.

In the first case, we have these nifty words called *contractions*, which are really two words rolled into one. In the second case, we need a way to show that a noun owns something. In both cases, we need an apostrophe. (Only nouns use apostrophes to show ownership. Pronouns don't. Instead, what we do with pronouns is create whole new words to show ownership, like *his, hers, theirs*—more on that later.)

The Apostrophe in Contractions

When you want to run two words together and create one quick word, you use an apostrophe to indicate some letters are missing. Instead of saying "It is my day off," we can shorten it is to "It's my day off." The apostrophe is just there to show the reader we're smart enough to know we left out the letter "i." It's critical to **put the apostrophe where the missing letters should be.**

Below is a list of some common contractions:

she's = she is *or* she has
let's = let us
won't = will not
he'll = he will

it's = it is *or* it has
doesn't = does not
they're = they are
who's = who is *or* who has

There are a gazillion more of 'em. The important things to remember are to put apostrophes in the right place and to make sure you really mean two words. Can you tell why the following sentence does *not* need an apostrophe in the word "its"?

In the book I'm reading there is a reference to a dog and *its* owner.

If I had put in the apostrophe, I would have been saying "the dog and *it is* owner," and that just plain doesn't make sense. As a general hint, when you're wondering if you are writing a contraction (particularly for the tricky ones like *it's, who's, they're, you're*) say the original words aloud or in your head to see if that's what you want. If you don't, you probably want the pronouns of ownership: its, whose, their, your.

Name _____   Date _____

Exercise 4.4

Directions: Let's practice what we just learned. In the following sentences, circle the correct word. Remember, say the contraction aloud to test whether or not you need an apostrophe.

1. (*It's, Its*) flavor is delicious when (*it's, its*) ripe.

2. (*Who's, Whose*) been eating all the Halloween candy?

3. (*You're, Your*) eyes look bloodshot . . . what have you been doing?

4. Paul (*is'nt, isn't*) happy when he (*doesn't, dosen't*) win every game.

5. (*You're, Your*) notified by mail if (*you're, your*) the winner.

6. Donny and Matt have devoted (*their, they're, there*) lives to the study of basketball.

7. (*It's, Its*) light goes on when (*it's, its*) overheated.

8. (*They're, Their, There*) mother worries whenever (*they're, their, there*) late.

9. (*Let's, Lets*) close the window if it (*let's, lets*) in too much air.

10. (*Who's, Whose*) mother is the lady (*who's, whose*) driving us to practice?

11. (*They're, Their, There*) usually sold before (*they're, their, there*) in the store an hour.

12. Mahin (*can't, ca'nt*) relax unless (*you're, your*) relaxed.

13. "(*You're, Your*) a wonderful teacher," said the student who hoped to gain favor in class.

14. (*It's, Its*) fur is thick.

15. (*They're, Their, There*) house burned down in a suspicious fire.

That was the easy part of the apostrophe. Let's forge ahead to the place where this stuff gets a bit more complicated.

Apostrophes Showing Ownership

Remember what was mentioned above? Apostrophes of ownership are used only with nouns. When a pronoun owns something we use new words to show possession, and they do not require apostrophes.

Examples	**His** car still has that great "new car" smell.
	Their house was built just last year.
	Her friend is a Buddhist.
	Ours is a unique country.

The boldfaced words are all pronouns of ownership. Now, let's look at what happens when the owner is indicated not by a pronoun, but a noun.

Grammar, Mechanics, and Usage

Name _____   Date _____

Possession with Singular Nouns

Don't be afraid of all those English-teacher words. All we're talking about here is what happens when one noun owns something. Somewhere back in the recesses of our mind we remember being told that with ownership we need to use an apostrophe, but we can't remember where it goes. Is it *before* the "s" or *after* it? Many indecisive souls solve this problem simply by placing the apostrophe on top of the letter "s." That way they look as if they know what they're doing, but in reality they're just copping out. Well, no more. Today you're going to figure this problem out. Let's get going.

When one noun owns something, the basic rule is: Add 's.

Examples	The **boy's hat** is blue. (The hat *of the boy*—that's what we're really saying.)
	My **friend's house** smells like dirty diapers. (One friend, one house—which happens to have a distinct odor.)
	Amelia's books are falling off the shelf. (Here we have one girl—Amelia, who happens to own many books, but we still use just the 's because the noun is singular. After all, one person can own many things. Remember the basic rule: **if the noun is singular, use 's.**)

In each of the above examples we're really using the 's so we don't have to use the phrase "of the." It's really an easier, faster way of saying *the house of my friend or the books of Amelia*. The apostrophe is a short cut, but like all short cuts it occasionally includes bumps in the road.

One little complication with the rule: What happens if the singular noun already ends in the letter "s"? For instance, what if we know someone named Charles who happens to be a big spender with many gadgets? Well, you've got one of two choices. You can say

Charles's unnecessary gadgets   OR   Charles' unnecessary gadgets

Both are correct. The first one is more common, but most textbooks indicate the second is more correct. Actually, what the grammar "bibles" say is something like this: "To show the singular possessive form of a noun of *one syllable* ending in an *s, x, ch,* or *sh* sound, write *s's*. However, if the noun is *more than one syllable* and ends in those same letters, add only the apostrophe (s')."

Possession with Plural Nouns

Sometimes more than one noun can own something. Usually a plural noun already ends in s, so the rule is simple:

Grammar, Mechanics, and Usage

Name _____ Date _____

When a plural noun owns something or several things, just add an apostrophe after the *s*.

Examples	The **babies' diapers** were fully loaded.
	(Obviously I'm back at the friend's house with the odor problem, and this poor caregiver has more than one baby with a diaper problem. I can tell because it's not "*the baby's* diaper" (which would mean only one baby), but it's the "*babies'* diapers.")
	Both speakers' comments were greeted with applause.
	(Again, I have more than one speaker. That's obvious because "speaker" ends in "s." But if you weren't 100% sure, the word *both* is the dead giveaway that there's more than one person exciting this crowd.)
	Several girls' boyfriends stood them up for the prom.
	(More than one girl had this problem.)

A complication for this rule: Sometimes plural nouns don't end in "s." In that case, flip back to the first rule and just add 's.

Examples	The **children's** game ended up as a free-for-all on the playground.
	(It's not just one child's game, but the *game of the children* that's wreaking havoc. Since the plural of child is "children," and that word doesn't end in "s," we just add 's.)
	The **women's room** at the local ballpark needs to be repainted.
	(Since this is a public facility that doesn't belong to just one woman, we need to use the plural, "women," and so we add 's.)

One More Bit of Advice: After an intense review of apostrophes, students often begin using an apostrophe whenever they see the letter "s." DON'T DO THAT! Remember, sometimes you have sentences with just plain old plurals in them. You use apostrophes with the letter "s" only when the issue of **ownership** is involved. The following sentence does not need any apostrophes. Why?

The girls rode their bikes to school.

Before placing an apostrophe before or after the letter "s," always ask yourself: "Is something being owned here?" You check yourself by inserting the phrase "of the" between the noun and what you think is being owned.

Grammar, Mechanics, and Usage

Name _____ Date _____

Exercise 4.5

Directions: Let's practice some of these apostrophe rules. First of all, let's make sure you understand the basic concept of ownership by turning the following phrases into possessives. Form both the singular and plural possessive of each expression. Make both nouns plural in the plural possessive. Explain to a partner what each phrase means. The first few have been done for you.

Example	Singular Possessive	Plural Possessive
1. the studio of the artist	the artist's studio	the artists' studios
	(one artist, one studio)	(the studios of many artists)
2. the hope of the man	the man's hope	the men's hopes
	(something one man wants)	(the hopes of many men)
3. the belief of the family	_____	_____
4. the hoof of the ox	_____	_____
5. the flag of the country	_____	_____
6. the earring of the teacher	_____	_____
7. the magazine of the woman	_____	_____
8. the skill of the player	_____	_____
9. the desk of the child	_____	_____
10. the toy of the baby	_____	_____

Grammar, Mechanics, and Usage

Name _____ Date _____

Exercise 4.6

Directions: Now you're going to really strut your stuff. This next practice exercise isn't an easy one, but it can be done. In the following story, 32 apostrophes are needed to show possession and to indicate contractions. Many of the words in this story will tempt you to insert incorrect apostrophes, but don't be fooled! You can do this; just slow down and think. Have fun!

Big Business

After working in our schools lost-and-found department for some time, Im astonished at peoples carelessness with their belongings and surprised at the publics honesty in returning things that arent theirs. When articles are found around the school, theyre usually brought to our fourth-floor office. We take each finders name, and if after a 60-day wait the article isnt claimed, the finder may keep it as his or hers.

We search each purses contents to find the name of its owner, but often theres no identification to be found. Occasionally a boys or girls picture, someones letter, or a drivers license will help us locate the owner. We cant help wondering what could have been in students minds when they brought to school and lost such unusual articles as a cows tooth, a pack of ping-pong balls, a suitcase filled with ladies hats, a rabbits foot,

and even a babys bottle. What must teachers assignments have been to bring forth such peculiar articles? It stimulates ones imagination!

At the end of the year when schools about to close for the summer, many dollars worth of unclaimed boys and girls clothing is turned over to the Helping Hand Societys collection box. Weve often wondered how its possible for someone to lose a perfectly good polar-fleece jacket, which probably cost a good deal of his own or his parents money, without even noticing its loss or bothering to check out its possible resting place. Its a mystery, too, why a student buys an expensive lifetime pen yet makes no effort to recover it when its lifes work has barely started. Oh well, at least it all makes for some good stories my friends and I can laugh about!

Grammar, Mechanics, and Usage

Name _____   Date _____

Quotation Marks

These really are not difficult marks of punctuation to master as long as you remember their most important and most used function: **Use quotation marks to record the EXACT WORDS someone has spoken.**

Example	"I still believe in the tooth fairy," responded the eight-year-old desperately trying to hold onto childhood.

These are the EXACT words that child said. But notice what happens below:

Example	She said that she still believed in the tooth fairy, but it was hard to believe when her room was filled with posters of the newest teen idol.

Even though the word *said* is used in that second example, it is not used to introduce the EXACT words she spoke, so I don't enclose anything in that sentence with quotation marks.

Once you have that concept down, the biggest issue with quotations revolves more around commas, and you may want to go back to page 70 to refresh your memory about where to use them when working with quotes. Below are a few simple rules to use when using quotation marks and other marks of punctuation:

1. **If a direct quote is a complete sentence, begin it with a capital letter. If it's just a fragment, don't use the capital letter.**

Examples	I heard Adam say, "Why yes, of course, I'd like a bite of that apple."
	Adam is reported to have said the apple left a "bitter taste in my mouth."

2. **When a quoted sentence is divided into two parts by an interrupter like *she replied* or *John pleaded*, the second part begins with a small letter. However, if the second part of an interrupted quotation is a new sentence, it does begin with a capital.**

Examples	"I'll take two whoopie pies," she began, "and four doughnuts, six eclairs, three lemon bars, and a loaf of whole-wheat bread to be on the healthy side."
	"Leave me alone," he begged, "or I'll tell my mom."
	"Don't stay out too late," Mother advised. "Remember, he was just released from prison last week."

NOTE: Go back and look at how the commas are used to set the quoted material off from the rest of the sentence. Again refer to page 70 for the explanation of how and where to place commas with quotation marks.

Grammar, Mechanics, and Usage

Name _____ Date _____

3. **Place periods and commas *inside* the quoted expression.**

Example	"You must take a deep breath before beginning your dive," the swimming coach instructed.

4. **Put question marks and exclamation points inside the quotation marks if they are part of the quoted matter. Put them outside the quotation marks if they serve to punctuate the entire sentence.**

Examples	She asked, "Are we too late?" "We're too late!" she shouted. Why did she ask, "Are we too late"? (NOTE: In this example the question mark really belongs with the first part of the sentence, so that's why it's on the *outside* of the quotation marks.)

5. **Quotation marks often set off slang words and other unusual expressions.** (NOTE: The period and comma belong inside the quotation marks.)

Examples	Gus' family always referred to him as "the problem child." Small shorebirds, often called "peeps," migrate early.

6. **Place semicolons and colons outside quotation marks.**

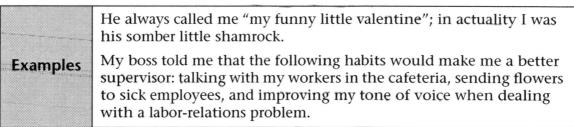

Examples	He always called me "my funny little valentine"; in actuality I was his somber little shamrock. My boss told me that the following habits would make me a better supervisor: talking with my workers in the cafeteria, sending flowers to sick employees, and improving my tone of voice when dealing with a labor-relations problem.

7. **When you're writing extended dialogue in a story, begin a new paragraph every time the speaker changes.**

Examples	"I love you to bits," Ernestine whispered into Frank's ear, "and even if you don't feel the same I'll still continue loving you." "But I feel the same way about you," Frank quickly responded. "In fact, do you know when I first realized I was falling in love?" "Tell me," Ernestine begged. "It was that day on the beach when I realized you had the same kind of sunglasses as I do. That's when I knew our fates were sealed."

Grammar, Mechanics, and Usage

Name _____   Date _____

8. Quotation marks are used to enclose the titles of chapters in a book, articles in a magazine, short stories, poems, songs, and other smaller works. Titles of books, magazines, plays, long poems, and other longer publications should be underlined when handwritten and italicized when printed.

Example	In last month's *National Geographic* there was an interesting story entitled "The Gold in the Tombs."

 Exercise 4.7

Directions: Copy the following sentences onto your own sheet of paper and insert quotation marks and any other required punctuation as needed. This is serving as a bit of a review of end marks, commas, and apostrophes as well as quotation marks.

1. Do you think Jerry asked that you will go to Macys or Filenes to do most of your holiday shopping

2. Michael also known as Mike is a friendly guy

3. Mother began by saying its your fathers opinion and I happen to agree with him that you need to have your own room.

   Youre kidding I quickly responded do you mean I no longer have to share a room with Ferdinand

   Yes that's exactly what we mean mother replied

4. when will we arrive in port the passenger asked

5. he said that he had once read A Tale of Two Cities but it must have been a long time ago because he couldn't even remember the main characters name.

6. Eleanor weve won the sweepstakes shouted Franklin pack your bags were heading to the Bahamas

7. Do you know the significance of the date april 25 1912 the history teacher asked his class

8. What she inquired have you done with the children

9. Because his first name was Fiorello Mayor Laguardia was known by those familiar with him as the little flower.

10. Finally the announcement came over the loudspeaker flight 1436 to Seattle and continuing on to Washington DC will begin boarding in five minutes.

Grammar, Mechanics, and Usage

Name _____   Date _____

Semicolons

Nothing can revolutionize your writing more than the proper use of semicolons.

Nothing.

However, like anything good, their overuse can minimize their effect, so what we're striving for with semicolons is a knowledge of how to use them in just the right places. Properly used, semicolons can make a reader sit up and really pay attention to what you're saying. That's what we're going after.

The Three Functions of a Semicolon

Function 1: Use a semicolon as a way to connect two sentences.

This mark of punctuation falls somewhere between the definitive finality of a period, the slight pause of a comma, and the gentle lull of the conjunction. That's the source of its power. When you are writing and come to the end of a thought, you basically have four choices:

1. Stop the sentence and put some end mark to indicate you're done. Then do the same for the next sentence.

2. Connect the two sentences by using a comma and one of the following coordinating conjunctions: *and, but, or, nor, for,* or *yet.*

3. Connect the two sentences with a subordinating conjunction like *after, although, because, since, when,* etc. (See page 27 for a complete list of subordinating conjunctions.)

4. Use a semicolon as a connection that's not quite as strong as a period, but more forceful than a conjunction.

Let's look at what I'm talking about:

Sample Paragraph—***Version #1***

It was time for my annual spring cleaning. The windows were first on my "to do" list. Hearing my mother's voice in the back of my head, I got out a bucket for the vinegar-and-water solution she always insisted was the best to use, and a few newspapers instead of the roll of paper towels I usually used. *Suddenly it struck me. I was becoming my mother.*

Version #2

After a while it struck me that I was becoming my mother.

Version #3

Suddenly it struck me; I was becoming my mother.

Can you feel a difference? Look at the underlined sentences. All of the versions of that paragraph are correct. There's nothing wrong with any of them. But there's a subtle difference between them. In the first version, the last two sentences have a definite break between the thoughts. In version #2, the connection is more "quiet" and gently joins the thoughts together. In version #3, the break is less severe than #1, but not as calm as #2, and as a result the reader sort of stops after the first thought and really pays attention to what's on the other side of the semicolon. You as the

Grammar, Mechanics, and Usage

Name _____   Date _____

author get to decide the "feel" you want. It's kind of like being a composer and deciding what kind of a finale you want. Do you want cymbals clashing and trumpets blaring to signify you're at the end? Do you want to go out with the soft touch of a lullaby? Or do you want your ending to blare those trumpets, play a rest note, and then crash the cymbals? That's what the semicolon does. It seems as if you've ended your thought, but then you give your reader the double whammy and really pack a punch with that last thought.

See if you think that's what's happening in the following examples:

Version #1: **Strangely, we loved that old tenement apartment. It was the place our life together began.**

Version #2: **Strangely, we loved that old tenement apartment because it was the place our life together began.**

Version #3: **Strangely, we loved that old tenement apartment; it was the place our life together began.**

Even more examples:

Version #1: **He no longer stood straight. Age had bent him.**

Version #2: **He no longer stood straight since age had bent him.**

Version #3: **He no longer stood straight; age had bent him.**

When using the semicolon for this function be sure you really have something powerful to say in the last part of your sentence. If you don't, the semicolon's effect is diminished.

Function 2: Use a semicolon before one of the following words when they are being used as transition words linking two independent clauses together: *for example, for instance, moreover, nevertheless, furthermore, otherwise, therefore, however, consequently, besides*.

Examples	The movie we saw last week was great for the most part; however, it moved a little slowly in the middle.
	I arrived 10 minutes late for the train; consequently, I had to wait over an hour for the next one to arrive.
	Sonya is planning on making the Olympic skating team; therefore, she practices night and day.

Function 3: Use a semicolon between items being listed in a series if the items themselves already contain commas.

| **Example** | The contestants for the pie-eating world championships came from Geneva, Switzerland; Hoboken, New Jersey; Sydney, Australia; and Montreal, Canada. |

Grammar, Mechanics, and Usage

Name _____ Date _____

Exercise 4.8

Directions: Practice your new-found appreciation of the semicolon in the following sentences. Place a semicolon wherever you think one should go. A few sentences also need commas added. Rewrite the sentences using one of the examples on page 84 as a model.

1. A kiss is not a contract an engagement is not a marriage.

   _____

   _____

2. Panic filled the air when the alarm sounded the men didn't know if they'd ever see their loved ones again.

   _____

   _____

3. The committee included Louisa Barkes president of Concerned Citizens Felix Walk chairman of the Board of Trustees for Penvalley College Marguerite Johanssen CEO of Comtel Computers and Rob Wood president of Mutual Airlines.

   _____

   _____

4. Tension was high at yesterday's meeting however after the lunch break members of the committee seemed able to get down to the business at hand.

   _____

   _____

5. Holiday traffic has always produced an increase in accidents for instance during the recent Thanksgiving holiday 632 people were injured on Florida's highways.

   _____

   _____

These next few marks of punctuation are not as complicated as the ones in the first part of this chapter, so we'll just do a quick look at some of these less-used but still important punctuation tools.

Name _____ Date _____

Colons

There are really only two instances in which a colon is necessary:

1. **Use a colon when you're beginning a list of items, especially if you use the words *as follows* or *the following*.**

Examples	Melanie packed the following for her weekend trip to Grandma's: three stuffed teddy bears, eight pairs of socks, 14 trousers with matching shirts, a jump rope, six books to read, and a box of Devil Dogs.
	Dad posted the following note: no eating in the car, no talking in the car, and no sleeping in the car.

2. **Use a colon after the salutation of a business letter. (Use a comma after the salutation of a friendly letter.)**

Examples	Dear Sir: To whom it may concern: Dear Polly,

NOTE: Remember to use a colon when writing times, i.e., 1:00 p.m., 3:30 a.m., etc.

Dash

Somewhat like the exclamation point and the semicolon, the dash should not be over-used. It will lose its effectiveness if you always pepper your pages with it. Its basic job is to *indicate an abrupt break in thought*. When typing, use the hyphen key twice (--) to indicate a dash.

Examples	There was only one way to describe Billy—way cool!
	I wish I had told you this before—but then you probably weren't ready to hear it—I'm planning to join the circus.

Name _____ Date _____

Hyphen

1. **Use a hyphen (-) to divide a word at the end of a line.**

Example	When Gloria was depressed, and unfortunately that was pret-ty often, she'd paint her fingernails and drink lemon water all day.

2. **Use a hyphen with some compound words used as adjectives when they** *precede* **the word they modify, and in some words used with their prefixes.** Be careful with this, as many words that once needed a hyphen no longer do. This seems to be one of the places where the fluidity of language is most apparent.

	door-to-door salesman	BUT	a salesman who sells from door to door
	An after-school meeting	BUT	a meeting after school
	A well-dressed man	BUT	a man who is well dressed
Examples	Ex-president governor-elect all-star		
	e-mail	BUT	World Wide Web (Watch out for computer-related terms; they may be changing and will lose their hyphens as they become more accepted into the spoken language.)
	African-American man	BUT	a man who is African American

3. **Use a hyphen when you're writing the compound numbers from twenty-one to ninety-nine and with fractions used as adjectives.**

Examples	*Forty-two* flamingos floated far away.
	Their *seventy-fifth* wedding anniversary is almost here.
	A *two-thirds* majority is needed to overturn a presidential veto.
	BUT
	Two thirds of Congress is needed to overturn a presidential veto.

Grammar, Mechanics, and Usage

Name _____   Date _____

Parentheses

Use parentheses ( ) when you want to set off information that is not vital to a sentence. Unlike the dash, parentheses tend to *minimize* whatever it is they are setting off. Also use parentheses to enclose figures or dates in a sentence.

Examples	Doing some type of exercise daily (swimming, running, step-aerobics) has exhausted her.
	We will celebrate Peter's birthday (September 29) at the roller rink.

Capitalization

1. **Capitalize the first word of every sentence.**

Example	When the cruise ship takes off, Avi will be on it.

2. **Capitalize the first word in a direct quote.** (See page 80 for more on this.)

Examples	"Don't you dare leave without me," Avi told the captain.
	Then the captain said, "Do you have your papers in order?"

3. **The pronoun "I" is always capitalized no matter where it appears in the sentence.**

Examples	Can I go on that boat, too?
	No matter what, I plan to get a room with a porthole.

4. **Capitalize the days of the week, months of the year, and holidays.**

Example	The ship is leaving on Thursday, November 28, which happens to be Thanksgiving this year.

5. **Capitalize proper nouns and proper adjectives.**

   Don't capitalize the names of school subjects—except for the languages, since they are proper nouns. If a course, however, has its name followed by a number or its full name, then it is considered a proper noun.

Examples	I heard Dustin Hoffman is planning a cruise vacation, too.
	This Norwegian cruise ship is one of the most luxurious boats ever built.
	I'm planning on learning Italian while on board, unless of course they're offering History of the Renaissance. I love history.

Name _____ Date _____

6. Capitalize the names of important historical events and periods, special events, and the formal titles of documents.

Examples	The ship was built during the Vietnam War, but it gets yearly upgrades.
	We'll be on board just after the World Series.
	I hear this is the ship where President Nixon penned his Address to the American People when he formally resigned from office.

7. Capitalize the most important words in books, magazines, movies, plays, songs, paintings, sculptures, and poems. Remember to underline or italicize those titles.

| **Examples** | I'm planning on taking along *Dr. Spock's Guide to Well Baby Care,* along with several back issues of *Parents* magazine. |
| | I've heard while we're on board there's going to be a performance of excerpts from the play *Cats.* |

Something to Think About: Using several marks of punctuation you've just learned about, punctuate the following: (It will make sense, I promise!)

that that is is that that is not is not is that it it is

Exercise 4.9

Directions: The following paragraph has no punctuation. Please rewrite the following story on a separate piece of paper and insert the correct punctuation and capitalization.

i will never forget the day june 12 1965 my dad and i sat in the cheap blue grandstand seats high above shea stadium in queens new york silently watching the rain fall after two hours the rain stopped and the crew slowly took the tarp off the field yes the game would take place after all of course it would take some time to get the field ready and both the new york mets and san francisco giants would have to take batting practice before the game could begin

after we saw bud harrelson ed kranepool and my other favorite players take their practice swings the game was ready to begin gil hodges the mets manager and alvin dark the giants manager brought their lineups to the umpire then the mets took the field play

ball shouted the homeplate umpire it was now 2:45 pm almost two hours past the scheduled 1:00 pm start

do you think the rain will stay away my dad asked i'm not sure i nervously answered sensing my anxiety my dad offered to buy me a soft drink they have coke™ orange grape and root beer which would you like he asked i replied i like root beer the best however i feel like a grape soda today

as he got up to buy me a soda i realized it wasnt the soft drink the weather or the game that really mattered to me it was the company

Chapter 5: Tricky Grammatical Problems

Background Notes

Do not use this chapter with students who are struggling with the basics of grammar. The issues presented in this chapter are for higher-level students who are making more subtle grammatical errors. Instead of focusing on the required "absolutes" of good grammar, we're now shifting and looking at more stylistic issues. This chapter covers the often humorous mistakes that result from writing dangling, misplaced, or squinting modifiers, as well as problems with ambiguous and indefinite reference and parallelism. Stress to your class that they don't have to identify exactly what type of mistake a sentence contains. Knowing the difference between a dangling modifier and a misplaced one isn't all that important. What counts is that they be able to spot subtle mistakes, not name them—and eradicate them from their writing once and for all.

What to Do on Day One

Since the finer points of syntax and style can be tough to get across, it's fun to begin by showing students examples to see if they can spot the errors. While it's a good idea to start off this more difficult chapter with some of the comical results of modifier mistakes, you also want to stress that sometimes mistakes like these can be really serious. Mistakes that lead to a misreading of vital information can be critical in docu-

ments such as police reports, letters of reference, medical articles, and so forth.

Write the following sentences on the board to see if students can pinpoint the problems:

1. I spent all morning at the veterinarian's office with my German shepherd and my brother Pete. It turns out he has worms. (Who has worms—the dog or the brother?)

2. One of the students told the teacher she didn't understand the lesson. (Who doesn't understand the lesson—the teacher or the student?)

3. My dad bought a computer for our whole family which he was unable to pay for, we later found out. (Was dad really unable to pay for the family?)

4. Walking up the path to the house, the bouquet placed in the bay window looked beautiful. (Wouldn't you love to see a bouquet walking up the path to your house?)

5. The president told the terrorist he needed to stop his atrocities. (So, who's committing terrible acts—the president or the terrorist?)

After you've had a few chuckles, warn students their mistakes will become fodder for classroom humor if they write sentences like these. Students often learn more from mistakes made in their own papers, so it's

(continued)

90

Chapter 5:
Tricky Grammatical Problems *(continued)*

a good idea to begin a file of student errors that can be used as an additional exercise.

Especially for ESL

Since our ESL students are still struggling with the basics of word placement and correct verb tense, this chapter can be tough for them. To lighten things up a bit see how many ways they think an English sentence can be written. Write each word from one of the example sentences on an index card. Shuffle the index cards so that the words are all out of order. Working alone or with a partner, students can put the words in the right spot to produce a logical English sentence. This is also a good approach to use for your kinesthetic learners whose first language is English.

Chapter 5: Tricky Grammatical Problems

If we could simply put our hands on our readers' foreheads and transmit our thoughts directly into their minds, we'd be doing exactly what we think we are doing when we write. We believe our ideas are so clearly written that every single person who reads our work should be able to understand exactly what we wish to convey.

That's where the problem comes in. We know what we want to say. In fact, we're sure we said it. But something often happens in the transmission of the message. We hand out our finished work to our very best friends and that strange look comes over them as they read. They don't know how to tell us that our writing doesn't make sense.

What's wrong? Sometimes the problem is simply that we're trying to explain very difficult ideas, and we get bogged down in our own words. Let's face it, anyone trying to use mere words would have a problem explaining something as complicated as quantum physics or the sociopolitical effects of World War II.

But sometimes we don't explain even simple ideas clearly enough. Often the problem is that we get our words out of order. The meaning of most English sentences depends largely on word order, so the position of each word becomes critical to clear communication. Choosing just the right words and placing them in precisely the right spot can help us write exactly what we want to say.

Watch what happens when phrases and clauses aren't right next to the words they're describing:

Examples	Give the desk to Ms. Mifflin with the thin legs.
	(Who has the thin legs—Ms. Mifflin or the desk?)
	Discouraged by low grades, dropping out seemed like the only logical thing to do.
	(Who was discouraged by low grades?)
	Lorenzo just died with his cowboy hat on.
	(Is the emphasis on the fact that Lorenzo died, or on the fact that he was wearing a hat at the time of his death?)

We think we know what we've said. We think it's crystal clear. But we sometimes forget we must place our modifiers **as close to the words they're modifying as possible**. Let me put that in English:

When you have one word or a group of words (e.g., a phrase or clause) describing something in a sentence, be sure that the word or group of words is *right next to* the words it describes. It doesn't matter if you memorize the following common types of "placement" mistakes; just be sure you can recognize when a sentence has a word-placement problem so you will not make these mistakes yourself.

Grammar, Mechanics, and Usage

Name _____ Date _____

Dangling Modifiers

A modifier in this case is a group of words that describes (modifies) another word in the sentence. A modifier is said to *dangle* when there isn't any word right next to it to modify. It's as if the writer left out the person or thing the modifying words are supposed to be describing. Take a look:

Unclear: All alone in the house, the sound of the howling wind petrified him. (You sort of get what's going on in the sentence. You know there's some boy or man who's all alone and scared of the noise. But the word order suggests that the sound of the howling wind was left all alone in the house.)

Clearer: All alone in the house, Eliot was petrified by the sound of the howling wind.
(Now we know who was alone and what he was feeling. *All alone in the house* is the modifier for *Eliot*; therefore, *Eliot* comes just after the modifier.)

Unclear: Having Hephzibah Schleribeck for a name, people have made me an easy target for raucous laughter and I've been on the receiving end of many jokes.

Clearer: Having Hephzibah Schleribeck for a name, I have been an easy target for raucous laughter and I've been on the receiving end of many jokes.

OR

Since I was given the name Hephzibah Schleribeck at birth, I have been an easy target for raucous laughter and on the receiving end of too many jokes.

You can be as creative as you want and add all sorts of words. Just be sure you use a comma if you start off with a descriptive phrase. That comma tells you that the next word in the sentence should be the person or thing you've just described; otherwise, you have a dangling modifier.

 *Exercise 5.1*

Directions: On a separate piece of paper, rewrite the following sentences to eliminate the dangling modifier. Remember, you will have to add some words and punctuation to make the meaning clear.

1. To run efficiently, the mechanic should oil the engine well.

2. After sitting there a while it began to snow.

3. Coming into the ice arena, the sound of the roaring crowd told Eli his team had just scored a goal.

4. The evening passed very pleasantly, eating candy and watching videos.

5. While racing along a deserted stretch of highway, two deer suddenly appeared in front of our car.

Name _____   Date _____

Misplaced Modifiers

Misplaced modifiers can turn a serious sentence into a joke. They become separated from the word they are intended to modify and end up modifying a different word entirely—often to comic effect. Usually you don't have to add any words to correct mistakes like this, you just have to move words around to clarify your meaning. Sometimes these mistakes are hard to pick up in your own writing because you think you know what you said. Just go back and be sure the order of each word expresses exactly what you intended.

Unclear: L.L. Freen, Inc. accepts returns from honest-looking customers of any size.

(Do you see the problem? Is it the customers of any size, or the returns of any size that L.L. Freen accepts? The modifier *of any size* is separated from the word it should modify *returns* and instead modifies a different word *customers*, thus changing the meaning of the sentence.)

Clear: L.L. Freen accepts returns of any size from honest-looking customers.

Unclear: Mr. LaTorre explained why plagiarism is wrong on Friday.

(So this is something bad to do only on Fridays? Tuesdays are all clear, right?)

Clear: On Friday Mr. LaTorre explained why plagiarism is wrong.

 Exercise 5.2

Directions: In the following sentences, correct the misplaced modifiers by placing the modifier right next to the words being described. You may use a separate piece of paper.

1. The dentist sent me a bill for the teeth she had filled by mail.

2. The mystery has been solved after 12 years of the missing socks.

3. At the picnic Duane served corn chowder to hungry guests in paper cups.

4. Rev. Howells announced that next Sunday's sermon would include an explanation of the nature of sin, which he hoped the congregation would be interested in.

5. Barbara prepares lavish lunches complete with soup, salad, and desserts just for her friends on Monday.

         Grammar, Mechanics, and Usage

Name _____   Date _____

Squinting Modifiers

Squinting modifiers are much like misplaced modifiers. The only difference is you've got a group of words that have been placed in such a way they could describe either the words before them or after them. Some books call them *two-way modifiers* since they can be applied to two parts of the sentence. Look:

> Ian said **on the top of the mountain** the view was breathtaking.

Did Ian say something like "this view is breathtaking" on the top of the mountain, or is he describing how the view looked from his position when he was on top of the mountain? The italicized words could be describing either the first part of the sentence or the second. You have to decide and move some words around. Here's what you'd come up with:

> On the top of the mountain, Ian said the view was breathtaking.

> OR

> Ian said the view was breathtaking on the top of the mountain.

Another example:

Not clear: Jody wanted to know before Carl went to practice who would do the laundry.

Clear: Before Carl went to practice, Jody wanted to know who would do the laundry.

Clear: Jody wanted to know who would do the laundry before Carl went to practice.

 *Exercise 5.3*

Directions: In the following sentences, correct the squinting modifiers in the two ways they can be rewritten.

1. I agreed on the next day to help Leslie with her homework

    _____

2. The boy Diane questioned solemnly shook his head.

    _____

3. Mom asked us before we went to college to call her on Sundays.

    _____

4. Tell Lois since she has the keys I want to see her.

    _____

5. Julia said at the mall Carmen acted silly.

    _____

 *Grammar, Mechanics, and Usage*

Name _____   Date _____

Parallelism

The issues we have tackled so far in this chapter revolve around making sure our ideas are written clearly so there's no chance of misunderstanding. That's not easily done, but now that you've seen some of the common pitfalls you should be on the lookout in your own writing for these easily made errors. This next problem, though, is a more sophisticated grammatical problem. It involves making sure your writing is smooth and free-flowing with no places for your reader to jump back and say "huh?"

Sometimes when you're writing a complicated sentence it's easy to get mired in your own words. There needs to be a pattern, or an order to your sentence so that the structure of the phrases and clauses is the same. When that happens the ideas in the sentence are connected correctly and your sentence is said to be in **parallel structure**. (This is as close to math class as we grammarians like to get. Remember parallel lines? They are a pair of lines that will never meet and help provide the orderliness mathematicians love so much. We English types just stole their idea and applied it to words.)

Sometimes this is more easily explained by example. Even if you can't quite give the technical, grammatical reason, you can probably "feel" that the following sentences are uneven:

David enjoys swimming and likes to play.

Rebecca seems interested and pays attention.

She asked for his name and where he lives.

In the sentences above, the word "and" is the connection point between the two parts of the sentence. To be completely parallel, the words on the first side of the "and" need to be stated the same way as they are on the other side of the "and." The way those sentences are written right now you can probably tell the words don't match up. You may not know exactly why, but you know it sure doesn't sound exactly right.

Now look at these next four sentences and see if you can pinpoint the place where the parallel structure falls apart:

The inmates were accused of robbery, assault, and forging checks.

The forecast was for snow in the morning and for it to be sunny in the afternoon.

Few of the dancers were as interested in improving their technique as they were in how much more pay they could get.

He says he can raise the needed funds for the school library by either organizing a bottle drive, or he will persuade his wealthy friends to contribute.

Could you feel the place where you began to feel off balance? You have to figure out the established pattern in the first part of the sentence and make sure you use the same one in the second half of the sentence. Nouns must be balanced with nouns, prepositional phrases with prepositional phrases, and clauses with clauses.

Grammar, Mechanics, and Usage

Name _____ Date _____

Let's look at how we'd correct the examples:

Faulty   **Parallel**

David enjoys swimming and likes to play.   **David enjoys swimming and playing.**

(The first side sets up the *subject-verb-gerund* [word ending in *-ing*] pattern, so we must use a gerund, not an infinitive, on the second side. It might help to silently repeat the entire pattern in order to decide what part of speech the second part of the sentence requires: David enjoys swimming and [*David enjoys*] playing.)

Rebecca seems interested and pays attention.   **Rebecca seems interested and attentive.**

(Here we have *subject-verb-noun* on the first side of the "and," so we had to find a noun that means "pays attention" to make the sentence structure parallel. The word *attentive* fills the bill. Rebecca seems interested and [*Rebecca seems*] attentive.)

She asked for his name and where he lives.   **She asked for his name and address.**

(Again, all I needed was a noun that means "where he lives" to give balance. She asked for his name and [she asked for his] address.)

To correct a sentence with faulty parallelism, you often need to *add new words* to complete the pattern. That's the fun part. You get to find the right words to make the rhythm stay true.

Let's keep analyzing the sample sentences:

Not Parallel   **Parallel**

The inmates were accused of robbery, assault, and forging checks.   **The inmates were accused of robbery, assault, and forgery.**

(Here we have a *series of nouns*, so we had to change the verb and noun "forging checks" into one simple noun—"forgery.")

The forecast was for snow in the morning and for it to be sunny in the afternoon.   **The forecast was for snow in the morning and sunshine in the afternoon.**

(This sentence begins with *subject-verb-two prepositional phrases* ["for snow," "in the morning"]. Each prepositional phrase ends with a noun; therefore, the prepositional phrases in the second part of the sentence must also end with a noun, not a verb and adjective. We must replace "to be sunny" with "sunshine." Notice, we don't have to repeat the preposition *for* because the meaning is clear.)

Grammar, Mechanics, and Usage

Name _____ Date _____

Few of the dancers were as interested in improving their technique as they were in how much pay they could get.

Few of the dancers were as interested in improving their technique as they were in getting more pay.

(This is a sentence of comparison—the first pattern has the preposition "in" followed by a gerund and then a two-word comparison, so on the second side we needed to find a gerund and another two-word comparison.)

Your approach to parallelism should be to figure out the pattern in the first part of a sentence and then to make sure you repeat that pattern in the second part of the sentence. The result is a clear, balanced sentence.

NOTE: Occasionally you do need to repeat an article, preposition, or pronoun to make the meaning of the sentence clear.

Example	While in Africa, Antonio took photographs of a gazelle and antelope.
	(It almost sounds as if there is one animal called a *gazelle and antelope*; therefore, it's better to make that phrase "of a gazelle and an antelope" so nothing is misunderstood.)

You do not always have to repeat articles, prepositions, and pronouns, but if you fear there could be any confusion on your reader's part, play it safe and sound repetitive.

 Exercise 5.4

Directions: Rewrite the following sentences to establish parallelism.

1. Broadway's newest production was lavish but a disappointment.

2. He left his home without a penny and after he had lost all his friends.

3. I like receiving letters much better than to write them.

4. Wharton's first novel was praised more for its style than for what it had to say.

5. To gain entrance to the backstage area of the concert hall, they tried both persuasion and to force their way in.

6. Come to the town meeting tonight prepared to take notes and with some questions to ask.

7. As Patrick grew older, he was torn between his love for his parents and his children.

8. As a result of the accident, Nelson had a broken wrist, several broken ribs, and one of his lungs was punctured.

9. Myles likes to wrestle, ride bikes, and many other sports.

10. The new neighbors soon proved themselves to be not only friendly but also people who could be counted on.

        Grammar, Mechanics, and Usage

Chapter 6: Stronger Writing Through Stronger Grammar

Background Notes

Here's where the fun really begins. Assuming your students have a working vocabulary of grammatical terms, you can now use the language of grammar to point out problems in their writing. Instead of saying something vague like, "This sentence seems a bit weak," you can now instruct your students to put more power into their verbs or use a gerund phrase to begin a sentence to add variety to their writing.

This chapter offers some concrete suggestions for improving writing. It covers the ways in which knowledge of the parts of speech connects to writing, and lists several ways to play with the usual subject/predicate pattern of sentences. It also includes exercises that encourage students to practice with sentence variety.

Questions to Ask Students

What are some of the characteristics of writing produced by second- or third-graders? What are the characteristics of good writing? How do you get from one extreme to the other?

What to Do on Day One

Introduce the 12 sentence patterns outlined below:

1. Begin with the subject.

   The storm began slowly.

2. Begin with a prepositional phrase.

   In the beginning of the storm, most people weren't worried.

3. Begin with an adverb.

   Slowly the storm built in power.

4. Begin with a gerund.

   Worrying about problems a storm can create won't help during the actual event.

5. Begin with an infinitive phrase.

   To prevent the panic a hurricane can create, people need to stay calm.

6. Begin with a present-participle phrase.

   Preparing in advance for all possible emergencies, people can know they've done all they could.

7. Begin with a past-participle phrase.

   Worried that he'd lose his house, Arthur did everything he could to safeguard it from the powerful winds.

8. Begin with an adverbial clause.

   Wherever a hurricane lands, destruction is sure to follow.

9. Use an appositive.

   Hurricane Gloria, one of the most powerful storms to hit the eastern seaboard, took the lives of dozens.

(continued)

Chapter 6: Stronger Writing Through Stronger Grammar *(continued)*

10. Ask a question.

    Is there any way to prevent the tragedies a hurricane brings?

11. Use an exclamation.

    Beware the fury of a Pacific storm!

12. Use conversation.

    The governor warned, "Do not stay in your homes, but go to an established shelter."

Discuss how each of these sentences has the same topic but forces the writer to think of new ways to introduce it. For each pattern, come up with a second sentence, which the class should develop together. Or, use a different topic and generate 12 new sentences.

For homework, ask the students to write a paragraph of at least six sentences on a topic of their choice (or provide a few options: e.g., my favorite hobby; what I did on my summer vacation; etc.) Tell them they MUST limit themselves to using only one sentence pattern. Pattern number 1 ("begin with the subject") is the most common, but tell students they can select one of the others if they want.

The next day see if you can get any students to share their paragraph with the rest of the class. Discuss what happens when the rhythm of a paragraph remains static.

For homework that night have them rewrite that same six-sentence paragraph, conveying the same basic information as the first; but this time they MUST use at least *four* of the patterns in their paragraph.

The contrast between the two paragraphs will undoubtedly be remarkable and obvious to every student. This exercise is a good springboard for discussing sentence variety and the other issues in this chapter.

Thoughts to Share With Students

All writers have their own style and voice. You want to encourage your students to find theirs. The more they write and play with the patterns of English the more they will discover a way to make their words flow in a way that feels right to them.

Especially for ESL

Many ESL students are desperate to learn how to write "perfect" English. They beg you to correct each and every mistake. Have them consider the possibility of an "immigrant voice" that's uniquely their own. Oftentimes there's a certain beauty, almost a poetry, to the sentences ESL students write that I believe should not be "corrected" and made to fit our patterns.

Name _____   Date _____

Chapter 6: Stronger Writing Through Stronger Grammar

The most important thing grammar can do for you—in fact, the only thing it can do for you—is make you a better writer. Now that you understand the grammar "shorthand" writers talk in, I can use grammar-talk to make some global statements about how to improve your writing. Without having to do a lot of explaining, I can use this chapter to give you a few tips to make your writing much more expressive and alive.

Making the Parts of Speech Work for You

Whenever you write, you put your knowledge of the parts of speech to use. Here are some specific guidelines.

1. Pay attention to the nouns and verbs you use.

The pulse of every sentence begins to beat with the nouns and verbs you use. Verbs inject power into your writing; nouns inject stability. Therefore, you want your nouns and verbs to be as *specific* and *concrete* as possible. Read the following pair of sentences and notice the different "feel" you get as the verb and nouns change:

1. The horse ran her last race.
2. The filly thundered down the stretch to the end of her career.

Both sentences describe the same event, but the second sentence is much more vivid because the nouns and verb are more defined. That's what you want to do. You want to give your reader the clearest possible picture of what's going on in your mind, and focusing on specific, concrete nouns and verbs helps you do just that. Sometimes, it's true, there's not much you can do to jazz up the nouns and verbs, but at least work towards this goal when you can to give your writing more energy.

Look at a few more examples to get this idea down.

Vague:	The children played outside at recess.
Specific:	Vanessa, Nicole, and Miranda bounded towards the monkey bars when they were set free from the classroom.
Vague:	The couple enjoyed the movie.
Specific:	Eric and Liz oozed with delight over *Titanic*.

Name _____   Date _____

 *Exercise 6.1*

Directions: Rewrite the following sentences using specific nouns and verbs.

1. The immigrant felt out of place.

   _____

   _____

2. The thief went into the bank.

   _____

   _____

3. The girls got a new haircut.

   _____

   _____

4. The telephone kept on ringing.

   _____

   _____

5. The runner trained for the race.

   _____

   _____

2. **Use active-voice verbs as often as you can. Use passive voice only when you have good reason to.**

You already know verbs can show either action or how something is existing. All verbs fall into one of those two categories. Now here's another thing about them: They can also be labeled as being in either **active** or **passive voice**.

Verbs in the **active voice**:

1. Must be action verbs.

2. Must have a direct object.

3. Must show an action that a subject does.

Verbs in the **passive voice**:

1. Must be state-of-being verbs.

2. Must have a subject that receives action from the verb.

Name _____ Date _____

That's the technical way of defining the guidelines for active and passive voice. What I really mean is whenever you can, make the subject of your sentence DO something. You don't want wimpy subjects. The following sentences should clarify this issue for you:

    Active voice: Frank eats chicken fingers for dinner on Fridays.

(We can easily tell the verb is an action verb [*eats*], and we can see the direct object [*chicken fingers*]; but the real proof that this sentence is in the active voice is that the subject is in motion—Frank eats.)

    Passive voice: The chicken fingers were eaten by Frank every Friday.

(Here we have a state-of-being verb [*were eaten*]; now the subject [*chicken fingers*] is receiving the action, not *doing* the action. The chicken fingers aren't doing anything except getting consumed by this guy every Friday night.)

 Exercise 6.2

Directions: Practice changing the following sentences from passive to active voice:

1. After the dinner was served by Patti, it was polished off by Kent.

    _____

    _____

2. The shenanigans of his trip to Atlantic City were described by Jim.

    _____

    _____

3. The babysitter was exhausted by the rambunctious children.

    _____

    _____

4. The long driveway was shoveled by me.

    _____

    _____

5. The drink was spilled all over the table by Nelson.

    _____

    _____

3. Use vivid adjectives and adverbs, but don't go overboard with them.

So often people think they can make a description clearer by sprinkling in more adjectives and adverbs. It's true, adjectives and adverbs do add spice to writing because by their very definition they're descriptive. Like spices, however, adjectives and adverbs should be used wisely; too many are as bad as none at all. Mashed potatoes without any salt taste like bland mush, but if there's too much salt you can't eat them either. Use adjectives and adverbs—and when you do, use vivid ones—just don't make every sentence a 35-word feast! You're not being paid by the word.

Which sentence on the next page is most effective?

Name _____   Date _____

1. It was a boring party.

2. As the lanky teenager sauntered into the gala, he could sense a stale, stultifying atmosphere enveloping the languorous crowd.

3. When Gregory arrived at the party he immediately sensed it was a snoozer.

All three sentences describe a party, but as Goldilocks in *The Three Bears* might say, the first one is "too dry," the second is "too much," and only the last one is "just right."

Think like Goldilocks when you write. You need some adjectives and adverbs in a sentence to heighten the specifics, but don't go overboard.

Exercise 6.3

Directions: Use what you now know about nouns, verbs, adjectives, and adverbs to rewrite the following sentences. Make them sparkle.

1. Our team was defeated by its rival.

   _____

   _____

2. Sharon was sad when her dog bit the babysitter.

   _____

   _____

3. Erin was scared by the thought of taking her college entrance exams.

   _____

   _____

4. The bird was bathed by Timmy.

   _____

   _____

5. George worked hard all his life.

   _____

   _____

6. Jason's rock group was good.

   _____

   _____

7. The girl was afraid of snakes.

   _____

   _____

8. The car was driven across country by Jean.

   _____

   _____

9. The masterpiece was painted by Kenny.

   _____

   _____

10. The cat wanted to eat.

   _____

   _____

Name _____   Date _____

The Games Writers Play with Subjects and Predicates

There's a distinct pattern to written English. Sentences typically start with the subject and are followed by the predicate. The truth is, aside from sentences that ask questions, it's hard to break that pattern. Unfortunately, if we don't, there is a monotonous rhythm to our writing that becomes almost predictable; trust me, that's one thing you don't want to be. Shake up what you're writing by making it look as if you're placing the predicate, or some of the action, first. Look at the following suggestions and use them to change the beat of your own writing.

1. Start some sentences with phrases.

You can make it *look* as if you're starting a sentence with its predicate first by throwing in a few phrases at the beginning of a sentence.

Example	**Having been at college for three months, Bethany found it hard to readjust to her mom's rules at home.** Someone could see those words "having been" at the start of the sentence and say, "Hey, I know a verb when I see one, so this must be the predicate of the sentence." Wrong. That introductory phrase is telling us more about Bethany, so it's actually part of the subject.

Example	**In the middle of the night Mike heard the baying of a nearby coyote.** This sentence starts with two prepositional phrases that tell us when Mike hears that frightening sound. In reality, those two phrases are part of the predicate because they modify the verb *heard*, and so the predicate *appears* to come first but it actually doesn't.

2. Start some sentences with dependent clauses.

Because dependent clauses have a verb in them, they can make a sentence look as if it begins with the predicate.

Example	**When she was a senior, Ana traveled to Hungary as an exchange student.** That introductory clause explains more about Ana as an exchange student. It could be tacked onto the end of the sentence, and then we would clearly see that actually it's part of the predicate. But who cares? By putting it at the beginning, which is just as correct, we're breaking up the typical pattern.

     Grammar, Mechanics, and Usage

Name _____ Date _____

Example	**After the earthquake leveled the village, the Red Cross appeared on the scene.** Again it *feels* as if we're focusing on the action first—the leveling of the village—but in reality, the sentence starts after the comma and follows the typical subject-predicate pattern. But the way it's written here makes the pattern look just the opposite.

3. Start sentences with verbals.

If the power of a sentence lies in its verb, start with a verb first, even if in reality that verb is now acting as a noun or adjective. Most readers won't know that. It can be your little secret. Here's a quick review of the three kinds of verbals:

A. Gerunds

These are verbs that have "-ing" added to the end of them and now operate as nouns.

Example	**Running three miles a day is good exercise.** The subject of this sentence is *Running*, which means it has to be a noun, since only nouns and pronouns can be the subject of a sentence. But it sure looks and feels like a verb, doesn't it? Most readers would swear we've started this sentence with the predicate first, but we haven't.

B. Infinitives

These are verbs that have the word "to" in front of them and now act as either a noun, adjective, or an adverb.

Example	**To design your own home takes a skill most homeowners don't have.** Again, I've got something that looks like a verb beginning a sentence, but the pattern is still subject-predicate. "To design" becomes a noun, and the subject of the sentence.

Name _____ Date _____

C. Participles

Participles are actually a form of a verb. They end in *-ing, -ed, -d, -t, -en,* or *-n*. They act as adjectives in a sentence. When you put them in a phrase in the beginning of a sentence, you *appear* to be starting with the action (predicate) of the sentence first.

Example	**Hesitating at the top of the ski slope, Brittany knew it was now or never to conquer her fears.**
	That word "hesitating" is actually introducing a phrase that's describing Brittany, so it's an adjective. But it could easily be mistaken for the predicate of this sentence by some unsuspecting reader.

4. Start some sentences with an adverb.

Sometimes just using a one-word adverb can really throw a sentence in a new direction. Often it casts an almost poetic atmosphere into a sentence.

Example	**Slowly the night unfolded its mysteries.**
	Usually we'd put the adverb "slowly" before the verb "unfolded." By just starting with the adverb we've altered the "feel" of the sentence just enough to make the reader concentrate on how the action was being done.
	Carefully she opened the gift.
	Again, this is not much of a change from the normal way we'd write this sentence, but just the slight rearranging of a typical pattern can be enough to add variety to a string of sentences.

Name _____   Date _____

Exercise 6.4

Directions: Practice what you've been learning by rewriting the following sentences to look as if they begin with the predicate first. Use a separate piece of paper. In some cases you will have to combine the information from two sentences into one longer sentence. The first few sentences indicate what technique you should use, but with the last few, do whatever feels best to you.

Example	The beggar crouched in the doorway. He hid his box of pennies. *(participial phrase)* Crouching in the doorway was a beggar hiding his box of pennies. OR Hiding his box of pennies, the beggar crouched in the doorway.

1. Joanne's performance was praised after the concert in our school. (*prepositional phrases*)

2. Jim will play golf every day as long as he is able to draw breath. (*clause first*)

3. A caterpillar was crawling up Elizabeth's back. It was fat and yellow and fuzzy. (*gerund phrase*)

4. Napoleon hoped that he would conquer the world. (*infinitive phrase*)

5. The old man stopped in his tracks. He looked in both directions before proceeding. (*participial phrase*)

6. Textbook study alone is dry and limited. Class discussion can help bring any subject to life. (*dependent clause first*)

7. Todd was in such a hurry to get to play practice on time he completely forgot his script at home on the kitchen table.

8. We rode to the top of the Eiffel Tower. It was a scary experience.

9. Helen's book on the Holocaust was written so students could understand the horrors of that event.

10. Everyone can be disturbed when there are loud whispers in the room.

11. Paul had no excuse to give the teacher. He simply hadn't done his homework.

12. It is a valuable art to be able to use words effectively.

13. Our opponents scored three touchdowns during the last quarter of the game.

14. Calculus is a hard subject for most students. Students who are good in math often find it difficult.

15. Let's sit in the sun. The heat feels good on our backs.

Answer Key

Exercise 1.1 (p. 3)

1. Courtney—proper, concrete
   Walt Whitman Mall—proper, concrete
2. nation—common, abstract
   president—common, concrete
   time—common, abstract
   war—common, abstract
3. crowd—common, concrete
   team (home team would be acceptable too)—common, concrete
   overtime—common, abstract
4. Democracy—common, abstract
5. echoes—common, abstract
   silence—common, abstract
   auditorium—common, concrete
6. One third—common, abstract
   (concrete is O.K. too)
   staff—common, concrete
   favor—common, abstract
   contract—common, concrete
7. files—common, concrete
   fire—common, concrete
8. Love—common, abstract
   game—common, abstract
9. lion—common, concrete
   savanna—common, concrete
10. John—proper, concrete
    pity—common, abstract
    dog—common, concrete
    pooch—common, concrete
    home—common, concrete

Exercise 1.2 (p. 9)

P = Pronouns   A = Antecedent (when there)   N = Noun

1. P = who
   A = people, for the pronoun *who*
   N = people, Alaska
2. P = many, themselves
   A = cast, for *many*
   N = cast, film
3. P = I, my, I, it
   A = shirt, for *it;*
   (the others have no clear antecedent)
   N = shirt
4. P = which, one, you
   A = students, for *one;*
   (others have no clear antecedent)
   N = students
5. P = She, her
   A = Not clear
   N = sister
6. P = Most, each, other (If students say "each other" is one word, that's O.K.)
   A = Harvard's graduating class, for *most*
   N = class (Harvard's graduating class would be acceptable); *to succeed* is an infinitive phrase used as a noun, but don't expect anyone to get that one yet.
7. P = you, whose
   A = woman, for *whose*
   N = woman, purse

8. P = who, it, others, me, its

   A = people, for *who;* Internet, for *it* and *its*

   N = people, Internet, possibilities

9. P = Each

   A = students

   N = students, notebook, day, class

10. P = Few

    A = cars

    N = cars, highways

11. P = Everyone

    A = not clear

    N = snowboarding, rage, slopes

12. P = her

    A = Cecelia

    N = Cecelia, husband, airport

13. P = that, I

    A = not clear

    N = copy, magazine, library ("Local library" is acceptable.)

14. P = they, who, them

    A = Printers, for *they* and *them;* people, for *who*

    N = Printers, computers, people ("Day" or "every day" functions as an adverb here.)

15. P = Either, one (It is O.K. if a student considers that one word.)

    A = children

    N = children, camp

Exercise 1.3 (p. 11)

1. I
2. us
3. her
4. me
5. them

Exercise 1.4 (p. 13)

1. bounced
2. was present; arrested
3. ran; was being chased
4. are going
5. should have been; loves
6. is
7. will come
8. seems; is
9. had purchased
10. sped

Exercise 1.5 (p. 17)

Note: In some sentences there are more possible answers than those listed below.

1. *has growed* should be *has grown* OR changed to the simple past, *grew*
2. get; *lay* should be *lie*
3. *could not have fell* should be *could not have fallen;* acted; were
4. C (must have brought; found; should have been)
5. was convinced; *had stealed* should be *had stolen* OR *stole*
6. C (swam)
7. C (had known; had; would have gone)
8. *could have took* should be *could have taken;* wanted; *built* should be *build*
9. *seen* should be *have seen*
10. *should have wrote* should be *should have written*
11. C (hung)
12. *begun* should be *began;* had forgotten
13. *have* should be *has; don't know* should be *doesn't know;* can help
14. asked; *had did* should be *had done;* wanted
15. claimed; couldn't go; *had drank* should be *had drunk;* upset; suspected

Exercise 1.6 (p. 21)

1. taught; *know* should be *knew* OR *knows*
2. *advise* should be *advised*
3. *has being* should be *have been*

4. predict; *will had been* should be *will be*

5. *will be participate* should be *will be participating* OR changed completely to *will participate*

6. *had spoke* should be *had spoken* or changed completely to *spoke; was advise* should be *was advised*

7. swim should be *swims*

8. *are not suppose* should be *are not supposed*

9. is; can tell; *is get* should be *is getting* OR changed completely to *gets*

10. *been* should be *were* OR *had been*

11. built; *settled* should be *was settled*

12. *will have been teach* should be *will have been teaching*; retires

13. *was ask* should be *was asked*

14. *go* should be *will go*; gets

15. *had knew* should be *had known* OR changed completely to *knew; want* should be *wanted*

Exercise 1.7 (p. 22)

This paragraph could be rewritten in the past or the present. Correct verbs are indicated for both.

Past

used to work (if students just circled *used* as verb, that's O.K.); was; *go* should be *went; write* should be *wrote; fill out* should be *filled out; could heard* should be *could hear* OR changed completely to *heard; tremble* should be *trembled; shakes* should be *shook; fall* should be *fell*; annoyed; decided; blared; *am* should be *was*; stood; *will pound* should be *would pound* OR changed completely to *pounded; will see* should be *would see* OR changed completely to *saw*; walking (this is actually a gerund—a verb acting like a noun—here, but if students list it as a verb accept it for now); *find* should be *found*; would volunteer; to be thrown

Present

used to work should be *work; was* should be *is*; go; write; fill out; *could heard* should be *can hear*; tremble; shakes; fall; *annoyed* should be *annoys; decided* should be *decide; blared* should be *blare*; am; *stood* should be *stand; will pound* should be *pound; will see* should be *see*; walking (this is actually a gerund—a verb acting like a noun—here, but if students list it as a verb accept it for now); find; would volunteer

Exercise 1.8 (p. 24)

(*Note:* Things can get a little tricky with this exercise, or, to put a positive spin on this, you can choose to look at this exercise as a place to challenge your own notions about grammar. Sometimes words that normally look like nouns or pronouns can be used as adjectives. You'll have to decide if you want your students to call them adjectives, or if it's more important for your students to understand the basics of nouns or pronouns. You can't go wrong either way. You may want to point out that there's a case for both explanations. [Also, in some cases students must decide whether a noun is two words long or if the two words are an adjective and a noun, as in #8.] Is street an adjective describing corner, or is this a two-word noun? Chiclets and gum are also two nouns. See, grammar isn't quite so rigid after all, now is it?)

1. It's already been done, but you may want to point out that the word "her" can be called

   a possessive pronoun or an adjective here.

2. Brittany likes soap operas filled with (sultry) heroines and (swarthy) men.

3. Ann's blueberry muffins and sincere kindness helped me when I was sick.

("Ann's" could be considered a possessive noun or an adjective here.)

4. Out on the noisy playground the rambunctious children released their pent-up energy.

("Their" can also be called a possessive pronoun.)

5. Many people stood in hour-long lines to finally have their chance on Disneyland's thrill ride, "thunder Mountain."

(You decide if "their" is a possessive pronoun or an adjective and if "Disneyland's" is a possessive noun or an adjective.)

6. Cuban cigars are often illegally brought into this country.

("This" can be a possessive pronoun, or a pronoun used as an adjective.)

7. My aunt and his uncle are getting married someday.

(Both "my" and "his" could be possessive pronouns or pronouns used as adjectives.)

8. A small child stood on the Mexican street corner begging tourists to buy small packs of Chiclets™ gum from her.

9. This laboratory experiment is fun.

("This" can be a possessive pronoun or an adjective.)

10. Two loud crows woke me from my pleasant dreams this morning.

("My" and "this" can be pronouns or pronouns acting as possessive adjectives here.)

Exercise 1.9 (p. 25)

Feel free to point out that sometimes pronouns and nouns in the following are used as adjectives.

1. (Done on student page.)

2. The student ran home quickly.

3. Ly luckily landed a job with the state's largest insurance agency.

4. Mr. Nestleroth often returns to his very small hometown in Nebraska.

5. Finally, I accepted the reality that my father was never going to return home.

6. We went to a bean supper here last fall.

7. Kim gradually became accustomed to the warm winter in Kansas, but she never stopped missing Alaska's cold.

   ("Missing" is a gerund here and not part of the verb.)

8. Jason was a very smart boy.

9. Cece will soon return to Hawaii for a visit.

10. Ganya carefully unwrapped her birthday present and happily shared her candy with everyone.

Exercise 1.10 (p. 26)

(Remind students that sometimes nouns and pronouns can be used as adjectives, and two words operating together can be adverbs.)

1. N = hair, river, back ("Emilia's" could also be called an adj.)

   P = her (It's being used as an adjective here, so ADJ is also correct for this word.)

   ADJ = Emilia's, beautiful, red

2. N = runners, marathons, bodies

   P = Some, others, it, their ("Some" and "their" could also be called an adj.)

   ADJ = grueling (However, "Some" and "their" could be in this category too.)

3. N = dog, door (Students could make a case for "next door" being an adverb.)

   P = us

   ADJ = A, loud, annoying

4. N = thieves, burglary ("taking" is a gerund so technically it is a noun), masks, front, camera

   P = their (It could also be labeled an adjective.)

   ADJ = The, three, flawless, ski, security

5. N = Ali, massacre, Pakistan

   P = none

   ADJ = the, grisly

6. V = wait

   ADV = often

   ADJ = long, most, department

7. V = decided, would like ("Visiting" is a gerund, so it's used as a noun here.)

   ADV = Eventually, rather

   ADJ = the, interesting

8. V = like, filled

   ADV = generally

   ADJ = outrageous, amusement, loud, video, noisy, heaping, junk

9. V = was noticeable

   ADV = barely

   ADJ = facial (Hung's could be considered an adj. as well.)

10. V = cooked

    ADV = carefully, slowly

    ADJ = a, delicious

Exercise 1.11 (p. 27)

1. and
2. either, or
3. Because
4. Neither, nor
5. If
6. not only, but also
7. but
8. since
9. both, and
10. and, before

Something to Think About (p. 28)

1. "Under" is an adverb.
2. "Under" is a preposition.

Exercise 1.12 (p. 29)

1. at, of—(at the bottom,) (of the dam)
2. to, with, under—(to the beach), (with their surfboards), (under their arms)
3. from, to, from—(from Pennsylvania), (to California), (from college). *About* and *after* both function as adverbs here.
4. During, of, of, without, for—(During the height), (of the blizzard), (of Coloradians), (without electricity), (for more than two weeks)
5. Around, from—(Around the corner), (from our house)
6. By, of, at—(By the time), (of Cam's family), (at the hospital)
7. except—(except Sunday)
8. over, through—(over the river), (through the woods)
9. beside, with—(beside the fish market), (with her friends)
10. in, without—(in school), (without a girlfriend)

Exercise 1.13 (p. 30)

1. C = and

   P = By, on

   I = none

2. C = and

   P = to

   I = Hooray!

3. C = When, whether, or

   P = none

   I = none

4. C = and, not only, but also

   P = none

   I = Yippee!

5. C = none
   P = at, of, of
   I = none

Exercise 1.14 (p. 31)

1. N = student, grade, class
   V = earned
   ADJ = The, industrious, a, top, the
   PREP = in

2. N = baby, sister, life, parents
   PRO = That, his, their (all of these can be called adjectives, too)
   V = make
   ADJ = lively, hectic ("his" and "their" could be in this category as well)
   ADV = very
   PREP = for
   C = and

3. N = exams
   PRO = I
   V = am, are finished
   ADJ = glad, final
   I = Whew!

4. N = day
   PRO = they, it
   V = knew, would be
   ADJ = a, fun
   ADV = immediately

5. N = Victor, job, Maria
   PRO = he, one
   V = wanted, feared, would find
   ADJ = a, new, a, better
   ADV = never
   C = but

6. N = Somalia, Dirte, medicine, United States
   PRO = he, he
   V = left, found, could practice
   ADJ = the
   ADV = not
   PREP = in
   C = After

7. N = movie
   PRO = She, I
   V = went
   ADJ = the
   ADV = home, soon
   PREP = after
   C = and

8. N = raise, October
   PRO = They
   V = get
   ADJ = a
   ADV = usually
   PREP = in

9. N = Bob, day, night
   PRO = he
   V = works, jogs
   ADJ = the
   ADV = usually
   PREP = during, at
   C = Since

10. N = Dozens, backpackers, trek, Appalachians, equipment, backs
    PRO = their, their (could be labeled adj.)
    V = began
    ADJ = the, long, the ("their" could be here as well)
    PREP = of, through, with, on

Exercise 1.15 (p. 32)

1. verb
2. noun
3. adjective
4. adverb
5. preposition
6. these = pronoun or adjective; brown = adjective
7. pronoun
8. noun
9. adjective or pronoun
10. pronoun

Exercise 2.1 (p. 36)

1. S = Clarissa
   P = diligently washed my red car
2. S = (You)
   P = Stop screaming
3. S = Sen's memories
   P = haunted him even after leaving Vietnam
4. S = The faculty and administration
   P = decided to impose a "no hats allowed in class" policy
5. S = the students
   P = did object why
6. S = Rashid and Philip
   P = have been friends since kindergarten
7. S = I
   P = Recently visited Mexico
8. S = The last day of school
   P = is a reason to celebrate for most students
9. S = you
   P = were born where
10. S = The fire chief and police officer
    P = worked together at the crime scene

Infinitive Phrase Explanation, (p. 40)

Infinitive phrase = To go
Prepositional phrase = to the circus

Exercise 2.2 (p. 41)

1. on the shelf—prepositional phrase used as an adjective

   in the center AND of the library—prepositional phrases used as adverbs
2. over the fence, into the alley, AND around the corner—prepositional phrases as adverbs

   to avoid—infinitive phrase as noun. (It's the subject of the "understood" clause, "in order" to avoid being caught. "Being caught" would then become the verb of that clause and not a gerund phrase.)

   by the dog catcher—prepositional phrase as adverb
3. Fighting a severe stomach flu—participial phrase as adjective

   to school—prepositional phrase as adverb

   learning more—gerund as noun functioning as direct object

   about grammar—prepositional phrase as adjective
4. To make the basketball team—infinitive phrase as noun functioning as subject
5. to become a writer herself one day—infinitive phrase as noun functioning as direct object
6. drawing all over the wall—participial phrase as adjective
7. Driving a car at 16—gerund as noun functioning as subject of sentence (Some would call "at 16" a prepositional phrase acting as adverb.)

   in most states—prepositional phrase as adverb

8. to speak—infinitive phrase as noun functioning as direct object

  in front—prepositional phrase as adverb

  of large audiences—prepositional phrase as adverb

9. Leaping to her feet—participial phrase as adjective

  to the stage, for a volunteer, AND from the audience—prepositional phrases as adverbs

10. at the restaurant—prepositional phrase as adjective

  to wonder—infinitive phrase as noun functioning as direct object

Exercise 2.3 (p. 43)

1. I = My friend is an excellent cook
  D = who is Italian

2. I = the game was canceled
  D = Because it looked like rain

3. I = I want to visit Ireland someday
  D = since it's supposed to be a beautiful country

4. I = My favorite book is A Tree Grows in Brooklyn
  D = which was written by Betty Smith

5. I = The joy of schussing down the slopes outweighs the pain of forking over so much cash
  D = Although skiing is an expensive hobby

6. I = The family lives on the corner
  D = whose dog always roams the neighborhood

7. I = The car is a Porsche
  D = that I like best

8. I = he always makes new friends
  D = When Peter is on the playground

9. I = You are reminded of the effects of World War II
  D = Wherever you visit in Germany

10. I = you have no idea how much your life can change
  D = Unless you've been through an exercise program; when fitness becomes part of your everyday life

Exercise 3.1 (p. 48)

Students' answers will vary. You may want to have students write their sentences on the board to see if they are complete and if commas are correctly placed.

Paragraph illustrating fragments and run-ons in text, (p. 46)

(There is more than one way to fix up this paragraph. Below is just one way.)

During the holidays Uncle Frank came with gifts for the entire family. He brought a wristwatch for me and a new computer game for my sister. We just loved it when he came because he was our favorite uncle. If he lived with us every day, I'm not sure we'd appreciate him as much as we do now. I sure hope he knows how special he is to everyone in our family.

Exercise 3.2 (p. 49)

1. Steffi Graf *was winning* or *won* the tennis match.

2. My friends *have gone* to a dude ranch.

3. Steve's letter *was published* in *The Miami Herald.*

4. For two years Joan *was working* or *worked* as a word processor.

5. *Have* you ever *been* to San Francisco?

Exercise 3.3 (p. 51)

(There is more than one way to fix up the following paragraph. Below is just one way.)

My favorite childhood vacations were the trips my family took to the beach each year. I just loved being the first of my brothers and sisters to run into the water and begin jumping the waves. Even after repeated warnings from my mother, I just couldn't contain my excitement. I would run out into the frigid waters, and before I knew it I was way out to sea. Then I would hear my mother's voice. Usually I had drifted far away from my family's blanket, and I could tell from the nervous sound in my mother's voice that I had scared her. When I'd finally get back to her, she'd tell me to please try and pay more attention to where I was going. However, it didn't take long before I'd be way out in the deep waters again. Eventually she'd give in and insist on jumping waves with me. I think it was the only way she could be sure to know where I was. To this day, the sound of the waves makes me want to hold my mother's hand.

Exercise 3.4 (p. 52)

(Below is one corrected version of the paragraph, but there is more than one way to write it.)

It is often difficult to recognize fragments and run-ons in paragraphs because the sentences are close together and seem to make sense. Most writers just assume their readers know what they mean, and so they just keep on writing as if they were talking. It really helps to look at one sentence at a time. You can see the problems then if you're careful. How does it seem so far? Let's put a couple more sentences together and see if it is still making sense to you. You need to remember it's not the length of the sentence that matters or the placement of punctuation. It's whether the sentence has a subject and a predicate, and expresses a complete thought. As you write more and more sentences, you will see the difference in your writing. The important thing is to keep checking your work. Writing isn't easy, but there's a good feeling you get when you know you've expressed your ideas clearly.

Exercise 3.5 (p. 55)

1. houses—cost
2. cause—is
3. Everybody—is
4. Many—like
5. Cells—need
6. Somebody—was
7. lack—amazes
8. Both—have
9. They—were
10. One—drinks

Exercise 3.6 (p. 57)

1. Sam and his brothers—sleep
2. estate—was
3. Either (Either Friday or Saturday is also correct for subject)—appears
4. fruit—looks
5. Fifteen dollars—is
6. All—is
7. team—has
8. Two weeks—is
9. Barbara and the others—sleep
10. Neither (*Neither the CEO nor the sales manager* is also correct for subject)—is
11. Three fourths—plan
12. few—hope
13. Neither (*Neither Yuri nor Svetlana* is also correct for subject)—earns
14. Max and his cousins—celebrate
15. Thea or Kendra—is

Exercise 3.7 (p. 60)

1. *Girls* is the antecedent for *her.*
2. *Students* is the antecedent for *their*

3. *Nobody* is the antecedent for *his*, but this sentence should be rewritten.

   Because it was "Find Another Way to Work Day," nobody drove a car.

   (Accept other correct rewrites of this sentence.)

4. *Officers* is the antecedent for *their*.

5. *Anyone* is the antecedent for *he*, but this sentence should be rewritten.

   If anyone knows the best way to do this math problem, please tell me.

   (Accept other correct rewrites of this sentence.)

Exercise 3.8 (p. 62)

1. *I* is the subject of the dependent clause.

2. *Us* is the object of the preposition *for*.

3. *Women* is the antecedent for *we* and is the subject.

4. *Everyone* is the antecedent for the possessive pronoun *his*, but this sentence should be rewritten to avoid gender issues.

   All the people in the group hoped their number would win. (This is just one way to rewrite this.)

5. *People* is the antecedent for *us* and is an indirect object.

6. *Anybody* is the antecedent for *him* and is a direct object, but this sentence should be rewritten to avoid gender issues.

   Tell all the people I know hello for me. (This is just one way to rewrite this.)

7. *Her* is the object of the preposition *to*.

8. *I* is the subject of the dependent clause.

9. *Horatio* and *they* are predicate nouns and pronouns, and even though it doesn't sound right, it is.

10. *Anyone* is the antecedent for *she*, which is the subject, but this sentence should be rewritten to avoid gender issues.

    If you've ever seen a glacier you wouldn't be able to forget it. (Accept other correct rewrites.)

11. *Person* is the antecedent for *he*, which is the subject, but it should be rewritten.

    After people retire, they often move down south. (Accept other correct rewrites.)

12. *Each* is the antecedent for the possessive pronoun *her*, but it should be rewritten.

    All of the jurors have made up their minds. (Accept other correct rewrites.)

13. *Many* is the antecedent for the possessive pronoun *their*.

14. *Dominic* or *he* is the subject of the sentence.

15. *Pete* and *me* is the direct object.

Exercise 4.1 (p. 66)

1. She did not like living among the lizards and rattlesnakes.

2. How wonderful it must be to grow up on a warm, sunny island!

3. Oh my goodness! Did you see the new teacher?

4. What a great party this is!

5. Did I ever tell you my middle name?

Answer to Something to Think About (p. 68)

No comma is needed after Internet because we do not have *two* sentences joined by a conjunction. This is simply a sentence with one subject (He) and a compound verb (has access, is hoping).

Exercise 4.2 (p. 69)

1. It's often a great deal of work, but the holidays are usually worth the effort.

2. The signal was given, the control button was pressed, and the rocket burst into the sky on its first mission. (NOTE: The second comma is optional. It can be omitted.)

3. I never expected to see them again, but like bad pennies they returned the next day.

4. fine as is

5. Proper equipment is needed for sailing across the Atlantic, and an experienced crew is helpful.

6. The waiter brought a vegetarian omelet, hash browns, toast, (comma optional here) and coffee for breakfast.

7. fine as is

8. Hank went shopping, and for once he didn't buy anything.

9. fine as is

10. It was a cold, raw, dark, November day, but I loved it.

Exercise 4.3 (p. 72)

1. While Ashley was talking to Kevin, Jenna entered the room.

2. fine as is

3. Some of the students were eating, others were doing homework, (comma optional here) but most were just goofing off.

4. fine as is

5. Having sailed around the world twice already, Barney was looking for a new adventure.

6. When Kasia arrived from Poland, she found learning a new language and the new cultural rules overwhelming.

7. Kyle asked, "Maggie, will you go with me to the movie on Saturday?"

8. The poet e.e. cummings did not use capital letters, and his punctuation was frequently unconventional.

9. fine as is

10. Melanie moved to Richmond, Virginia, on June 1, 1997, and in 1998 she plans to move to Dallas, Texas.

11. Rock climbing has become a popular sport, and its popularity seems to be growing.

12. Behaving like a spoiled child, Frederick sulked until Edna gave in.

13. Sally's brother thought they should get two turkeys for Thanksgiving, since 28 guests were planning to come.

14. I like chicken, mayonnaise, (comma optional) and mustard on my sandwich.

15. fine as is

16. Hagos will, I am sure, let me borrow the car tomorrow.

17. While taking an afternoon stroll in the park, my little brother made friends with three squirrels, two elderly gentlemen, (comma optional) and a score of toddlers.

18. She is beautiful, in fact, stunning is more the word.

19. fine as is

20. "I began running at the age of 10," Aimee said, "but I got serious about training in high school."

21. fine as is

22. Frank got a job at the Hotel Continental, 443 Newbury Street, Boston, Massachusetts, for the summer.

23. fine as is

24. Lisa, one of my closest friends, recently moved out of town.

25. fine as is

26. For breakfast we had ham and eggs, orange juice, toast, (comma optional) and coffee.

27. My new friend Thung is hoping to find a job as an engineer, which is what she was in Cambodia.

28. fine as is

29. As we sat on the veranda of our spacious summer home, we wondered how we would ever leave the place.

30. "Yes, I'm talking to you," the angry mother informed her young son.

Exercise 4.4 (p. 75)

1. Its, it's
2. Who's
3. Your
4. isn't, doesn't
5. You're, you're
6. their
7. Its, it's
8. Their, they're
9. Let's, lets
10. Whose, who's
11. They're, they're
12. can't, you're
13. You're
14. Its
15. Their

Exercise 4.5 (p. 78)

3. the family's belief; the families' beliefs
4. the ox's hoof; the oxen's hooves
5. the country's flag; the countries' flags
6. the teacher's earring; the teachers' earrings
7. the woman's magazine; the women's magazines
8. the player's skill; the players' skills
9. the child's desk; the children's desks
10. the baby's toy; the babies' toys

Exercise 4.6 (p. 79)

Paragraph One: school's, I'm, people's, public's, aren't, they're, finder's, isn't

Paragraph Two: purse's, there's, boy's, girl's, someone's, driver's, can't, students', cow's,

ladies', rabbit's, baby's, teachers', one's

Paragraph Three: school's, dollars', boys', girls', Society's, We've, it's, parent's or parents' (it depends on whether the student thinks only one parent bought it or if both of them did), It's, life's

Exercise 4.7 (p. 82)

1. "Do you think," Jerry asked, "that you will go to Macy's or Filene's to do most of your holiday shopping?"

2. Michael, also known as "Mike," is a friendly guy.

3. Mother began by saying, "It's your father's opinion, and I happen to agree with him, that you need to have your own room."

   "You're kidding!" I quickly responded. "Do you mean I no longer have to share a room with Ferdinand?"

   "Yes, that's exactly what we mean," mother replied.

4. "When will we arrive in port?" the passenger asked.

5. He said that he had once read *A Tale of Two Cities* (students will underline), but it must have been a long time ago because he couldn't even remember the main character's name.

6. "Eleanor, we've won the sweepstakes!" shouted Franklin. "Pack your bags. We're heading to the Bahamas."

7. "Do you know the significance of the date April 25, 1912?" the history teacher asked his class.

8. "What," she inquired, "have you done with the children?"

9. Because his first name was Fiorello, Mayor Laguardia was known by those familiar with him as "the little flower."

10. Finally, the announcement came over the loudspeaker, "Flight 1436 to Seattle and continuing on to Washington D.C. will begin boarding in five minutes."

Exercise 4.8 (p. 85)

(There is more than one correct way to do rewrites. Accept the range of student responses.)

1. A kiss is not a contract; an engagement is not a marriage.

   Rewrites: A kiss is not a contract. An engagement is not a marriage.
                    A kiss is not a contract, and an engagement is not a marriage.

2. Panic filled the air when the alarm sounded; the men didn't know if they'd ever see their loved ones again.

   Rewrites: Panic filled the air when the alarm sounded. The men didn't know if they'd ever see their loved ones again.
                    When the alarm sounded, panic filled the air because the men didn't know if they'd ever see their loved ones again.

3. The committee included Louisa Barkes, president of Concerned Citizens; Felix Walk, chairman of the Board of Trustees for Penvalley College; Marguerite Johanssen, CEO of Comtel Computers; and Rob Wood, president of Mutual Airlines.

4. Tension was high at yesterday's meeting; however, (a comma is also acceptable before "however") after the lunch break, members of the committee seemed able to get down to the business at hand.

5. Holiday traffic has always produced an increase in accidents; for instance, during the recent Thanksgiving holiday 632 people were injured on Florida's highways.

   (Students should also have written three sentences using a semi colon.)

Answer to Something To Think About on (p. 89)

That, that is, is. That, that is not, is not. Is that it? It is!

Exercise 4.9 (p. 89)

I will never forget the day June 12, 1965. My dad and I sat in the cheap, blue grandstand seats high above Shea Stadium in Queens, New York, silently watching the rain fall. After two hours the rain stopped, and the crew slowly took the tarp off the field. Yes, the game would take place after all. Of course, it would take some time to get the field ready, and both the New York Mets and San Francisco Giants would have to take batting practice before the game could begin.

After we saw Bud Harrelson, Ed Kranepool, (comma optional) and my other favorite players take their practice swings, the game was ready to begin. Gil Hodges, the Mets manager, and Alvin Dark, the Giants manager, brought their lineups to the umpire. Then the Mets took the field. "Play ball!" shouted the homeplate umpire. It was now 2:45 p.m.(or pm) almost two hours past the scheduled 1:00 p.m. (or pm) start.

"Do you think the rain will stay away?" my dad asked.

"I'm not sure," I nervously answered. Sensing my anxiety, my dad offered to buy me a soft drink.

"They have Coke™, orange, grape, and root beer. Which would you like?" he asked.

I replied, "I like root beer the best; however, I feel like a grape soda today."

As he got up to buy me a soda, I realized it wasn't the soft drink, the weather, or the game that really mattered to me. It was the company.

Exercise 5.1 (p. 93)

(Each of the following is just one of the many ways these sentences can be rewritten. Accept a range of student answers.)

1. To run efficiently, the engine should be oiled well by a mechanic.

2. After sitting there a while, I noticed it began to snow.

3. Coming into the ice arena, Eli could hear the sound of the roaring crowd and hoped his team had just scored a goal.

4. Any evening can be passed very pleasantly if you eat candy and watch videos.

5. While racing along a deserted stretch of highway, we were shocked when two deer suddenly appeared in front of our car.

Exercise 5.2 (p. 94)

1. The dentist sent me a bill by mail for the teeth she had filled.

2. The mystery of the missing socks has been solved after 12 years.

3. At the picnic Duane served corn chowder in paper cups to hungry guests.

4. Rev. Howells announced that next Sunday's sermon, which he hoped the congregation would be interested in, would include an explanation of the nature of sin.

5. On Monday Barbara prepares lavish lunches complete with soup, salad, and desserts just for her friends.

Exercise 5.3 (p. 95)

1. I agreed to help Leslie with her homework on the next day.

   On the next day, I agreed to help Leslie with her homework.

2. The boy Diane questioned shook his head solemnly.

   Solemnly, the boy Diane questioned shook his head.

3. Before we went to college, Mom asked us to call her on Sundays.

   Mom asked us to call her on Sundays before we went to college.

4. Since Lois has the keys, tell her I want to see her.

   I want to see Lois since she has the keys.

5. At the mall Julia said Carmen acted silly.

   Julia said Carmen acted silly at the mall.

Exercise 5.4 (p. 98)

(Accept many different responses.)

1. Broadway's newest production was lavish but disappointing.

2. He left home friendless and penniless.

3. I like receiving letters much better than writing them.

4. Wharton's first novel was praised more for its style than for its content.

5. To gain entrance to the backstage area of the concert hall, they tried both persuasion and force.

6. Come to the town meeting tonight prepared to take notes and ask questions.

7. As Patrick grew older, he was torn between his love for his parents and his love for his children.

8. As a result of the accident, Nelson had a broken wrist, several broken ribs, and a punctured lung.
9. Myles likes to wrestle, ride bikes, and play many other sports.
10. The new neighbors soon proved themselves to be not only friendly, but also reliable.

Exercise 6.1 (p. 102)

(Accept a wide range of sentences that follow suggestions in the text.)

Exercise 6.2 (p. 103)

(Accept a range of answers.)

1. After Patti served dinner, Kent polished it off.
2. Jim described the shenanigans of his Atlantic City trip.
3. The ranbunctious children exhausted the babysitter.
4. I shoveled the long driveway.
5. Nelson spilled the drink all over the table.

Exercise 6.3 (p. 104)

(Accept a wide range of student responses that follow suggestions made in the text.)

Exercise 6.4 (p. 108)

(Accept a wide range of answers.)

1. After the amazing concert in our school, Joanne's performance was the talk of the town.

2. As long as he draws breath, Jim will play golf every day.
3. Crawling up Elizabeth's back was a fat, yellow, fuzzy caterpillar.
4. To conquer the world was Napoleon's hope.
5. Stopped in his tracks, the old man looked in both directions before proceeding.
6. Because textbook study alone is dry and limited, class discussion is what helps to bring a subject to life.
7. Hurrying to get to play practice on time, Todd completely forgot his script at home on the kitchen table.
8. Riding to the top of the Eiffel Tower was a scary experience.
9. So children could understand the true horrors of the Holocaust, Helen wrote a book geared specifically for that purpose.
10. Whispering loudly disturbs everyone in a room.
11. Sadly, Paul had no excuse to offer his teacher for not doing his homework.
12. Using words effectively is a valuable art.
13. By scoring three touchdowns during the last quarter, our opponents won the game.
14. Even students who are good in math find calculus a difficult subject.
15. Sitting in the sun feels good on our backs.